Margin of Life

MARGIN OF LIFE

Population and Poverty in the Americas

Photographs by

Cornell Capa

Text by

J. Mayone Stycos

GROSSMAN PUBLISHERS, NEW YORK 1974
in cooperation with
The International Fund for Concerned Photography, Inc.
and
The International Population Program—Cornell University

Recent books by J. Mayone Stycos:

Human Fertility in Latin America

Children of the Barriada

*Ideology, Faith and Family Planning
in Latin America*

Clinics, Contraception and Communication

Recent books by Cornell Capa:

Farewell to Eden (with Matthew Huxley)

Adlai E. Stevenson's Public Years

The Concerned Photographer 1 (edited)

The Concerned Photographer 2 (edited)

Behind the Great Wall of China (edited)

Language and Faith

Copyright 1974
in all countries of the International Copyright Union
by Cornell Capa and J. Mayone Stycos

First published in 1974 in a hardbound and paperbound
edition by
Grossman Publishers, 625 Madison Avenue,
New York, N.Y. 10022

Published simultaneously in Canada by
Fitzhenry and Whiteside, Ltd.

SBN 670–45618–7 (hardbound)
670–45619–5 (paperbound)

Library of Congress Catalogue Card Number: 72–90916

Printed in Belgium

DESIGNED BY ARNOLD SKOLNICK

Preface by J. Mayone Stycos

This is neither a happy nor a hopeful book. It was conceived out of my desire to place the Latin American population problem in the perspective of the many other serious problems facing Latin America, and to bring that message forcefully to Americans. To do the former I had to abandon the comfortable academic specialization to which I have grown accustomed, and try to see and understand the large web of problems facing poor countries. To do the latter I looked for, and found, a creative and socially conscious photographer who would not only take good pictures but who could help me see and understand.

Capa and I then approached the Rockefeller Foundation, where a felicitous combination of interests in science and the arts resulted in a grant which made our project possible.

We then chose Honduras and El Salvador as our demographic microcosm. They were about as small as countries go and therefore easier to cover and comprehend than large countries; but they had the main ingredients we were interested in: rapid population increase, poverty, and painfully slow progress in improving the lot of the average citizen. Most of all we chose them because they had just had a war whose roots were in poverty and population, and we wished to show that if it could happen to these small sister nations, larger ones might not be far behind.

We took several trips together to each of these countries, talked to and photographed hundreds of people. (All interviews were tape recorded, transcribed in Spanish, and translated into English by me.) We saw beautiful homes and beautiful people as well as hovels and poverty; and saw a good deal of joy as well as misery. We have chosen to emphasize the darker side of the picture because we feel it is both more representative and more demanding of attention. In so doing we risk disappointing many of the people in Honduras and El Salvador who gave us generously of their time and assistance, and we risk incurring the hostility of public officials sensitive about the national image. We regret this, but believe that in the long run we will have done more good than harm; for North Americans must know what Central America looks like after a decade of the Alliance for Progress, and there are also many Central Americans who need to know.

In photographing and writing about specific people and highly contemporary situations, we run an apparent risk of rapidly going out of date. Since the text was written, for example, El Campamento 3 de Mayo has been rebuilt, Modesto Dominguez has been released from jail, and El Salvador's progressive minister of education has been moved to a harmless diplomatic post. But the basic currents carrying these actors flow relatively undisturbed and the larger forces shaping the day-to-day situations go essentially untouched. It is these basic currents and larger forces which we are trying to illuminate by our down-to-earth examples.

Scholars, journalists, and photographers must probe, diagnose, and call attention to. We hope we have done this. We hope others will do what they have to do.

Ithaca, N.Y.

Contents

> "It's not the slums that are marginal,
>   It's the people, it's us...
>   We are on the margin of health,
>   The margin of education,
>   The margin of work.
>   We cry to the four winds
>   That we don't want to be marginal..."
> SLUM DWELLERS' PETITION TO CONGRESS

Introduction

Most of the countries of the world are both small and poor. We have chosen two of them—El Salvador and Honduras—to show what it means to be small and poor during a period of rapid population growth. It is essentially a story of the tenacity of life, of the struggle for existence by people who are the victims of a complex biological and social situation beyond their understanding or control. The pressures have spiraled within recent years to the point of eruption.

These two sister nations, culturally and ethnically so similar that it is difficult for a native of one to distinguish a native of the other, suddenly became the bitterest of enemies in 1969, and experienced a brief conflict, the viciousness of which left both sides astonished and embittered. This war has been termed "the soccer war," because of a game between the nations which helped to trigger the conflict; and it has been termed "the demographic war," because of the key role played by the Salvadorean migrants to Honduras. Neither name suggests reasons for brothers and neighbors to slaughter one another; it is important to understand such reasons, and in so doing, to point up the international risks of poverty.

POVERTY

How poor are these countries? The gross national product per person is $236 for Honduras and $280 for El Salvador. By this admittedly crude measure of wealth, the United States is 16 times as rich; Puerto Rico, 4 times; Mexico and Chile, twice. Ecuador and Guatemala are in the same economic category as Honduras and El Salvador, and India and Haiti are only one-third as wealthy. Sociologically speaking, they might be considered middle-lower-class nations.

What is it like to be a poor nation? Consider Honduras. Life expectancy there is 50 years; every other person is a child under 15. In a country where two out of three are farmers, two out of three farms are less than two acres. While the average Southern Negro family in the United States earned $4,000 in 1967 and only 7 percent earned less than $1,000, close to half of Honduras's rural families earned less than $250. In a nation the size of our poorest state, there are just over 300 miles of paved roads, as compared with Mississippi's 65,000. After a decade of the Alliance for Progress, Honduras has 43,000 students enrolled in primary and secondary school, and each year graduates 2,500 from high school. With approximately the same population but many fewer children, South Carolina has 650,000 enrolled and graduates 34,000 per year from high school. South Carolina has 4 times the number of physicians, 25 times the number of nurses, and 10 times the number of telephones.

El Salvador is somewhat better off, but not much. It has more

1
Poverty and Population

Most of the countries of the world are both small and poor. We have chosen two of them—El Salvador and Honduras—to show what it means to be small and poor during a period of rapid population growth. It is essentially a story of the tenacity of life, of the struggle for existence by people who are the victims of a complex biological and social situation beyond their understanding or control. The pressures have spiraled within recent years to the point of eruption.

roads, more doctors, more industry; but with a half million more people and only one-fifth the land area, and with a highly unequal distribution of wealth, Salvador's edge over Honduras diminishes in significance. Both countries depend on one crop for at least half their export earnings, half the adults in both nations were illiterate in 1960, and in both countries illegitimate births greatly outnumber the legitimate. The veneer of material superiority readily apparent in El Salvador's capital is a thin one, and it is scarcely evident in the rural areas.

POPULATION

Few Latin Americans are concerned about population control. Despite the fact that El Salvador has one of the world's highest rates of population increase and is among the most densely settled of the world's poor nations, one of its major dailies has carried on a pronatalist crusade for an entire decade, at a rate of almost one editorial per week. Napoleon Viera Altamirano, editor of *El Diario de Hoy* and an avid conservationist, maintains that Latin America needs at least 2 billion more people to achieve its destiny. "To populate America is to civilize America," he maintains, and accuses foreign interests of wishing to "dissect the wombs of Latin American mothers and castrate Latin males."

Altamirano reflects a brand of nationalistic *machismo* far more insidious than that celebrated in Sunday journalists' accounts of the lower-class male's fertility. While Altamirano's position may seem extreme, it reflects a feeling typical of Latin Americans— that for some ulterior motive, the rich countries are trying to treat Latin America for a disease it doesn't have. While the alleged motives range from genocidic through diversionary to palliative, there is one common thread: "We have no population problem."

This belief is based on a sketchy perception of three demographic dimensions: population size, density, and rate of growth. Central Americans understandably see their countries as *small*. Chicago, after all, has more people than Honduras and El Salvador combined. Secondly, they regard the number of people as few in relation to the land area. Honduras has only about 60 people per square mile—and if it is pointed out that El Salvador has 400, one often hears that Holland has a thousand and what's wrong with Holland?

In fact, however, the heart of the demographic problem lies in the rate of growth and its effects on the age distribution of the population. "The predominant feature of Latin American populations is its speed of growth," writes Carmen Miró. To this generalization, Central America provides a choice particular. Only fifty years ago the combined populations of Mexico and the six other Central American nations were less than the current population of New York State. By 1980, however, they will have multiplied between four and five times to reach a population the size of the United States in 1910 (see graph). Not only popula-

Population of Honduras and El Salvador, 1920–1980

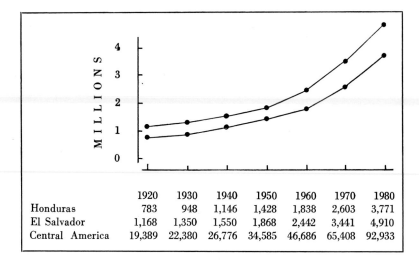

	1920	1930	1940	1950	1960	1970	1980
Honduras	783	948	1,146	1,428	1,838	2,603	3,771
El Salvador	1,168	1,350	1,550	1,868	2,442	3,441	4,910
Central America	19,389	22,380	26,776	34,585	46,686	65,408	92,933

SOURCES: Carmen Miró, "The Population of Twentieth-Century Latin America," in *Population Dilemma in Latin America* by J. M. Stycos and J. Arias (Washington: Potomac Books, 1966); CELADE, *Boletín Demográfico* 1 (Santiago, Chile, 1968).

tion but the *rate* of increase has been increasing. At the current rate of about 3.5 percent annually, El Salvador and Honduras are doubling every 20 years. Twenty-five years ago they were growing at about 2 percent, which doubles the population "only" every 35 years.

"The more the countries grow," writes demographer Jorge Arévalo, "the greater the portion of the national product which must be allocated to satisfy basic needs, such as education, with the result that the resources to be invested in economic development are scantier." High birth rates, however, lead to more than sheer population growth—they also bring about a population bottom-heavy with young people. Thus in Argentina, with a relatively low birth rate, less than a quarter of the population is aged 7–19, whereas in Honduras and El Salvador a third of the population is in these school ages. If the population increases of these nations were due to the immigration of young people seeking employment, as was the case during the period of the United States' most rapid growth, it would be less costly because of the favorable ratio of producers to consumers. But Central America's growth due to natural increase comes at a premium, because it increases both the number of dependents and their proportion in a population in which everyone is struggling to eat a little better and be a little better educated.

To see how this rate of growth has been achieved, we present a few figures from El Salvador, where registration of births and deaths is quite reliable (see Table A).

Even though El Salvador's population increase will be 2.5 million persons between 1946 and 1975, the number of deaths per year remains fairly constant, because mortality rates have been declining. But the birth rate remains high, and the number of births rises as the population increases. Thus, the population growth is the result of declining death rates and high but stable birth rates—a familiar phenomenon in poor countries where death control has preceded birth control. The net result is that while El Salvador was adding about 40,000 people per year in the mid-forties, it is currently adding about 120,000 per year, *and the number is rising every year.*

There is, moreover, an enormous difference in quality between the earlier and the later increase. In prewar Salvador, the worlds of the poor and the rich were very clearly demarcated. Hunger, ignorance, and disease were taken for granted as the lot of the poor, just as luxury, knowledge, and health were the prerogative of the rich. The poor were invisible to the rich. They did not vote, they did not complain, they did not move to the cities. So long as there were enough of them to harvest the coffee and tidy the houses, *it hardly mattered how many of them there were,* since each addition cost the nation nothing. But times are changing. The poor have begun to move to the cities, to organize sporadically, to complain, to vote, to demand schools, jobs, and hospitals. At the same time there are now planning boards, the Alliance for Progress, and a spirit of economic development. If knowledge, health, and employment are the right of everyone, then each addition to the population becomes very expensive, especially if the social benefits are not matched by productive employment. In short, not only is the number of people rising, but the unit cost is rising even faster. The combination is catastrophic to the poor nations already marked by slow increases in national product. The "obvious" solutions are to reduce the rate of population growth and to increase and redistribute the wealth. These are not alternatives—all of them must be achieved if the individual well-being of the citizens is to be improved. In the following chapters we will show, both in words and in photographs, how desperate the situation is; we will explore the complex intermesh of population and socioeconomic problems, and show how inadequate current efforts are to solve them.

Table A

El Salvador Natural Increase, 1946–1975

	Births	Deaths	Natural Increase
1946	72,000	31,000	41,000
1955	105,000	31,000	74,000
1965	137,000	31,000	106,000
1975 (est)	(184,000)	(31,000)	(153,000)

SOURCES: Statistical Office of the United Nations, *Demographic Yearbook 1957; 1965; 1968.*

Death control has preceded birth control.

While rates of death have declined, the number who die has not. The increasing density of population makes death more visible than ever.

2
Land

El Salvador has one of the highest percentages of land utilization in Latin America, according to the Inter-American Development Bank; about 95 percent of the national territory is under cultivation. With an average of 400 people for every square mile of territory, and with a growth rate that doubles the population every 20 years, what alternatives has an essentially agrarian society in which all the land is utilized? There are two: Either the people get off the land, or the land accommodates more people. In leaving the land, the people may either leave the nation altogether or relocate within the nation, normally in the cities. If they stay put, the accommodation can be made either by belt-tightening—the people accepting a lower standard of living—or by rearrangements in the land-holding system. In El Salvador everything but the last alternative has been tried.

El Salvador's economy shows the oscillations characteristic of the one- or two-crop economy typical of many Latin American republics. The annual growth in gross national product was 5.5 percent at the beginning of the 1950s, dropped to 1.2 percent in 1953–54, rose to 6.6 in the next four years, dropped to zero in 1958–59, rose to 7.2 in the early 1960s, and by the end of the decade was down to about 4 percent.

Coffee and cotton account for 55 percent of the nation's export earnings, and coffee alone accounts for a tenth of the gross national product. Indeed, tiny El Salvador accounts for 2.5 percent of the world's coffee production. But in recent years the world demand for coffee has been growing at only about 3 percent per year, while the supply has been growing at about 5 percent, driving the price lower and lower. Cotton production has been especially variable, with the cultivated area dropping from 100,000 hectares in 1963–64 to 43,000 in 1967–68. Needless to say, the best lands are used for such crops, along with large areas of land used for relatively primitive cattle raising. Plantation crops and cattle raising are largely controlled by big landowners, 145 of whom own a fifth of the land. At the other end of the scale are over 107,000 farms (or nearly half of all landholdings) of less than a hectare of land. In 1961, the owners of these farms were averaging an income of $25 a month. Even so, they were better off than landless workers, who averaged $19.

Large estate farming, of course, employs much less manpower than the same land could support in small farms, simultaneously aggravating both the employment problem and the domestic food problem. It also absorbs the best farm land, much of it in pasture waiting for prices or technology to change. With an abundant labor supply and low wages, the owner of a large farm needs to invest little in order to reap adequate profits.

Economist Jacques Chonchol explains how it works:

> In the large traditional estates which are the most typical and also quite often on the large modern plantations which rely

mainly on the cultivation of a single crop, we find an extra-ordinary degree of underemployment of agricultural land and labour. . . . For those who have available large land areas as well as an abundant supply of labour, extensive methods of farming are very advantageous. With the use of only small amounts of effort and capital—apart from the land—and very little risk, it is possible to obtain a personal income which is more than satisfactory from the point of view of the owner's economic and social requirements, and for his exercise of political influence. Frequently the total value of the wages paid on these large traditional-type estates represents less than 10 percent of their gross product. Moreover, an important proportion of these wages is not paid in cash but in concessions such as the temporary assignment of a marginal plot of land for the worker's own crops or the right to graze a few animals on the estate's pastures. This enables the landowner to carry on the productive process without the necessity of relying on any appreciable amount of working capital, while exerting social and political power over the peasant attached to his estate as a result of the concessions granted to him.

Everything, indeed, tends·to accentuate the desire and urge to accumulate land which, by virtue of the political influence of the owners, pays only a minimum in the way of taxation, and tends to maintain a high real value in the midst of the continuous monetary devaluation process of many of the Latin American countries. In addition, this system results in the land remaining as natural pasture or being subjected to a minimum of agricultural use: its value is greater as a source of personal income, social prestige and political power than as a factor of agricultural production.

El Salvador is justly proud of its recent gains in industry, which have helped to give it a high rate of overall economic growth during most of the 1960s. However, 60 percent of the population relies on agriculture for its living, and this, as flatly expressed by a recent Nathan Associates report, is "where the country failed. From 1950 to 1967 the economy grew at a real rate of 5.2 percent per year, but agriculture averaged 2.9 percent, and since 1962 has slackened to about one percent."

The decline in agricultural production has not been matched by a decline in population. While it is true that the proportion of farmers in the total population is declining, *their number is rapidly increasing.* There were, in fact, 71,000 more persons working in agriculture in 1961 than in 1950 despite the rapid exodus to the cities, and the Salvadoran Planning Board estimated that 100,000 *more* would be working in agriculture in 1969 than in 1961.

The net result, according to the Nathan report, is far too many people working on farms: "An unofficial estimate suggests that the total agricultural labor force is fully employed only an average of 125 to 180 days a year." Daniel Slutsky, an economist at the University of El Salvador, calculates that either "190,000 persons of working age in the rural area are totally unemployed or the working force is in fact only working about 168 days per year." One dramatic measure of the employment situation is seen by the 1961 census finding that just under a third of the nation's boys aged 10–14, as well as two-thirds of the men aged 75 and over, are "economically active."

The situation for the small farmer has been getting worse over the past two decades, as population has grown and land available for subsistence crops has shrunk. The deterioration was already evident in 1961, as can be seen from comparison with the census of 1950 (see Table B).

While there was virtually no increase in the number of holdings of three hectares or more, there were over 50,000 more small holdings in 1961 than in 1950. Moreover, while the number of renters of land increased by 147 percent, the number cultivating their own land *decreased* by 18 percent.

The small farmer was becoming not only smaller and more dependent, but hungrier. If we take the principal food crops—corn, rice, and beans—we find virtually no change in annual production in the first two between 1950 and the mid-sixties, and a marked decline in the production of beans. Since population almost doubled in this period, the per capita production of foodstuffs showed marked decline. While food imports increased, given the deterioration in size of land holdings and the high degree of agricultural unemployment, it is almost certain that the farmer was eating less.

What about agrarian reform? As early as 1950 the Rural Colonization Institute was created and authorized to acquire and prepare rural property for subdivision. Some notion of the speed of its operation can be gathered from the fact that between 1962 and 1966, in the heat of Alliance for Progress land reform fervor, it awarded 3,198 plots of land during a period when El Salvador's rural population grew by about 200,000. In 1970 even the gentle Committee on the Alliance for Progress (CIAP), in reviewing El Salvador's annual report, had to say that it "considered it highly important that the programming of agrarian reform be advanced in the near future with great speed."

As for the future, the government seems to be relying on industry. As it stated in the Five Year Plan of 1965–69: "The relative scarcity of agricultural lands and the growing population demand a high rate of economic development, based principally in the nonagricultural sectors. . . . El Salvador has no alternative to increasing its rate of industrial expansion, because of the limited opportunities for agricultural expansion." Even this somewhat desperate reliance on industrialization may have been shattered by the war with Honduras and the collapse of the movement toward economic integration of Central America.

Even if the urban population increases from its current level of 40 percent of the nation to 50 percent by 1985, the rural popula-

Table B		
El Salvador Land Ownership, 1950 and 1961		
	1950	1961
Number of land holdings	174,000	224,000
Number of land holdings smaller than three hectares	125,000	176,000
Average hectares per holding	8.8	6.9

tion is expected to have grown from its 2.1 million in 1970 to close to 3 million by 1985. In the light of these facts, El Salvador will have to come to grips with the conclusion reached by the Nathan report: "The country's future is undoubtedly linked to what happens in agriculture."

But to modernize agriculture in a traditional way could easily aggravate the employment situation unless the already rapid rural-to-urban migration is further *accelerated*. As agricultural economist Solon Barraclough expresses it: "Accelerated agricultural development alone cannot be expected to result in substantially improved incomes for most of the peasantry. Modernization of agriculture offers a solution only if many rural residents move to more productive urban jobs. A continuously growing productivity per worker is only foreseeable if new technology is introduced and the ratio of land and other resources per worker is vastly improved. In other words, accelerated migration from many heavily populated agricultural regions is a necessary condition for their continuous development."

As we shall see, El Salvador's industry, while accounting for a fifth of the gross national product, is not providing many jobs, and the cities are already bulging with unemployed. "Modernizing" agriculture in El Salvador without true land reform could only mean more belt tightening around already emaciated bellies.

"I'm a farmer. I grow corn and beans on one and a half manzanas of land which my father left me."

"How much land did *he* have?"

"About ten manzanas, but we were eight brothers, and each of us took a little piece."

"But what will all *your* children do?"

"Well, when you're poor you just have to put up with it. We can't do anything but work the land. We were never taught to read. The children, well, they may have to move to the city."

Modernizing agriculture without
true land reform can only mean
more belt tightening around already emaciated bellies.

The land has not increased but the people have. We don't fit any more. It is getting desperate.

ANDRÉS

. . . The poor run from one place to another to find a little piece of land to work. They risk having to stay without finding work in a new place. The landowner, if he wants to give to the poor he gives, and if not he does not give. If he wants, the land will not be worked. The poor man is enslaved. Because of his needs he subjects himself to all the injustices of the rich. . . .

PADRE ALAS

Signing up

Coffee and cotton account for 55 percent of export earnings, and coffee alone accounts for a tenth of the Gross National Product.

3
The War

As population increased and export crop agriculture expanded in El Salvador, the rural population began to move in two important streams—to the cities on the one hand, and across the border to Honduras, on the other. The trade links between the two countries were intensified by the Central American Common Market, with Honduran foodstuffs going to El Salvador, and manufactured products returning to Honduras. Salvadorans had migrated to Honduras in some numbers over the past two decades. In part this was encouraged by the agricultural export companies in Honduras—United Fruit and Standard Fruit—who considered Salvadorans highly desirable workers. It was also encouraged by Salvadoran entrepreneurs in cotton who found land in Honduras easy to rent or buy, and who then brought over Salvadoran workers for the harvests. Finally, many poor farmers who could not find land in El Salvador migrated in search of a plot big enough to provide for their families.

We visited a large camp of refugees who had been expelled from Honduras, and asked a number of the men why they had left El Salvador in the first place. Their replies were almost invariably of this kind:

> I had been renting about eight manzanas here. I had cows and oxen. But they sold the hacienda, and I could find no one to rent me land. It's terrible here.

> I went to Honduras six years ago because you couldn't rent land here.

> We were under the domination of the rich, we couldn't afford the rent they were asking for land.

> It used to be that the rich would rent you land and take part of the crop in return. Now they only rent to the cotton growers, not to the poor.

> I had to pay $24 per manzana rent for growing corn. In Honduras I rented land for $1.50.

> I rented about three manzanas at $20 each per year, and in addition I had to give the owner four sacks of grain per manzana, hardly leaving us enough to eat for the home. Then cotton came and you couldn't even rent at that price.

A survey of 140 heads of families temporarily located at the Santa Tecla Red Cross center showed that half had been unemployed at the time they left El Salvador and that three-quarters had worked their "own" land in Honduras. By the end of 1969, according to El Salvador's minister of foreign affairs, there were 250,000 Salvadorans in Honduras. Many if not most of these had entered illegally, and many were occupying national lands. The Honduran government had traditionally taken a permissive attitude toward the immigrants but was less inclined to do so as the immigrants grew in number and wealth. Moreover, while land was more plentiful in Honduras than in El Salvador, in a number of regions it was getting scarce indeed. The great scarcity in Southern Honduras is discussed in Chapter 11. Rodney Stares

I feel happy because it's the Day of the Republic. . . . Honduras, the great things it's done. . . . I feel moved. This country is great. It's not like El Salvador, the people are like sardines in a can there . . . a tiny country. But Honduras is big. It has lands, lands that nobody lives in.

ORANGE VENDOR

commented that the entrance of Nicaraguan and Salvadoran entrepreneurs in cattle and cotton tripped off enclosure movements in the south which evicted Hondurans just as they had in El Salvador:

> The experienced bought land in the South . . . and although the number of properties was small they seemed to have a demonstration effect. . . . It may have directly or indirectly been responsible for the enclosure movement. Perhaps newly arrived aggressive foreign farmers, becoming conscious of the increased value of having land reserves in the event of a general expansion of commercial agriculture, decided to extend their boundaries as a precautionary measure.

At the same time, it was becoming clear to Hondurans that the common market was doing much more for El Salvador than for them. From 1960 to 1967 Honduran exports to El Salvador doubled, but her imports from El Salvador increased five times, leaving a large deficit in the balance of trade. Her overall foreign debt increased from $18.5 million to $122 million in the same period. There began to emerge among intellectuals the uneasy feeling that Honduras was becoming El Salvador's colony in the traditional economic sense. Further, because of the common market, import duties which would have been levied on foreign manufactures were now lost—costing the nation about $20 million in 1967, whereas it cost the others about $10 million. As a result, there was an increase in internal taxes, which was partly responsible for strikes of teachers, railroad workers, and others. The goverment may have become concerned about its popular backing and might have been seeking a new rationale for a military regime. In any event, in 1969 the Agrarian Reform Institute began to take seriously earlier agrarian legislation which provided that only native-born Hondurans could own land which had belonged to the nation, or could obtain permission to form communal property in Honduras. Foreigners with large land holdings became the convenient targets for the first expropriations of land in a decade of agrarian reform, and small farmers began to be denied land if they lacked the appropriate credentials. As Salvadorans were expelled, border incidents began to develop, the press and radio jumped in to stir up nationalistic feelings, and a nasty incident at the soccer game between the two nations brought matters to a head in June, 1969. In El Salvador another dictatorial regime was having its own internal troubles and was not slow to react to an external threat. In both countries the press and radio whipped up nationalistic sentiments in what an OAS investigating committee called "an extremely aggressive attitude that has served to poison the spirit of these two peoples with hatred." Fabio Castillo, former rector of El Salvador University, commented that the crisis was fabricated to prop up both reactionary regimes. Commentator Aaron Segal concluded that

"each side sought to use the problem of the migrants as a tool to fortify national sentiment and silence or intimidate political opposition."

By mid-year, feelings of resentment were so high in El Salvador that President Sánchez had to act or fall. On July 14 Salvadoran Mustangs bombed Honduran cities in a "defensive strike," while Salvadoran troops invaded. The first war between Latin American states in 35 years was on. The OAS did not take long to arrange a cease-fire, and El Salvador removed its troops from Honduras on August 3. Casualties in human lives were not great, but there was a great residue of bitterness.

The economies of both countries were badly damaged. During the first half of 1970 Honduras incurred an $18-million trade deficit with Guatemala, Nicaragua, and Costa Rica because of her lost foodstuffs export market with El Salvador. While El Salvador was faring better on its exports, by mid-1970 it had at least a hundred thousand new mouths to feed and 35,000 new jobs to find for the refugees from Honduras. Both military regimes had been strengthened, and military spending increased markedly. Perhaps most significant of all, these tiny sister nations had learned to hate one another.

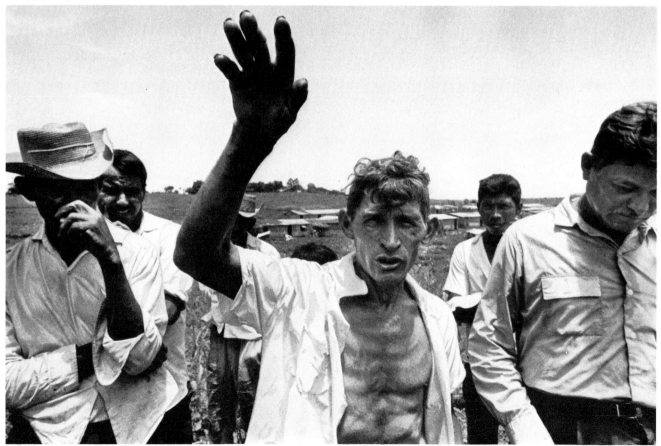

Jobs, Houses, and Schools

If it is true, as the Punta del Este Declaration to the Peoples of America declared, that the right to housing is a fundamental right in a democratic society, then most Latin Americans' rights are being abused. Although there are few Latins without roofs over their heads, the cardboard and thatch of which so many roofs are constructed are certainly not what the writers of the declaration had in mind. Almost a decade after the bold housing goals established by the Alliance for Progress were set, a report on housing in Central America published by the Organization of Central American States (ODECA) termed the situation "truly alarming" and confessed that "when the Bogotá charter was signed and the Alliance for Progress initiated, there was no clear picture of the magnitude of this problem."

In most Latin American countries the bulk of the population has lived in huts for centuries. As late as 1950, for example, close to three-quarters of the rural dwellings of Honduras, Panama, Paraguay, and Venezuela had earth floors. Such homes, if considered at all by urban dwellers, were regarded as "quaint" or as "natural to the simple country life." But toward the middle of this century the peasants began to move in force to the cities, and although their urban housing conditions were in many ways superior to those in rural areas, they suddenly became "deplorable." In fact, what had been invisible became visible, not only because the migrations were physically concentrated in the capital cities, but because the poor were suddenly under the very noses of the rich—so close, and in such numbers, that they could be not only seen but smelled.

In Rio de Janeiro the *favela* population grew from 400,000 in 1947 to over a million in the early sixties; in Lima the proportions of the city's population living in *barriadas* rose from 10 to 25 percent in two decades; Caracas and Bogotá grew at the incredible rate of just under 7 percent per year, most of it in shantytown areas. Pushed by the increasing unavailability of land and pulled by the lure of cash wages and a place in school for their children, the Great Peasant Trek had begun.

Housing rapidly became a problem. Based on the censuses of 1951, the Pan American Union concluded that there were 19 million dwelling units in Latin America "not compatible with human dignity, and which should be destroyed." Instead, during the fifties most of them were vacated by the older arrivals and eagerly rented by new arrivals fortunate enough to find a ready-made shack.

Initially the *hacendados* were pleased and the industrialists delighted. The large landowner felt no labor shortage because the rural labor force continued to grow at nearly 3 percent per year despite the emigration. Further, the city provided a safety valve for potentially hostile peasants displaced by mechanization or

4
The City: Jobs Houses and Schools

By packing many families into a small space and providing few utilities, the landlord can make a handsome profit from even the poorest populations.

rationalization of land use. For the urban entrepreneur the abundant labor force meant that the price of labor could be kept low for both the factory worker and the domestic servant, not to mention the multitude of service workers—shoe shiners, car washers, package carriers and messengers—who made life more agreeable. Indeed, life would have remained idyllic but for several facts. First, as the old slum areas in the center of the cities became inadequate to house the new poor, the migrants began to invade land at the periphery of the city. Paying exorbitant rents for the landlord's *mesones* in town was one thing; erecting one's own shack and living rent-free out of town was different. It was "invasion." Second, unlike the pattern of urbanization in Europe, where the early migrations were both a consequence of and stimulus to industrialization, industrialization in most Latin American countries never blossomed. Thus, what was in the beginning a delightful labor surplus soon became a glut of unemployed who began to cost money in urban social services. Moreover, once turned on, the urban migration could not seem to be turned off. Long after the demand had been exhausted, the rural supply, goaded by rising expectations, decreasing land availability, and increasing population, marched on.

As a result of this inflated level of urbanization, many Latin American countries give a false impression of belonging to the modern world. It is a fact that about 60 percent of Latin America's labor force is engaged in nonagricultural occupations —a level not reached by the United States until 1890. There is a very important difference, however. While the United States of 1890 had half its nonagricultural labor force working in industries, contemporary Latin America has less than a third. Most of the rest are in "services," a category which covers not only the bus driver and government clerk, but the prostitute, the household domestic, and the seller of lottery tickets. As explained by Raul Prebisch, former head of the Latin American Institute of Social and Economic Planning, the service sector "is bulging with redundant people who could be removed with no lowering of efficiency." And the service sector is growing rapidly. While the Latin American industrial labor force has been growing annually at 2.8 percent, service occupations have been growing at 3.8 percent, even reaching 5 percent in Brazil.

Within industry a large proportion of the jobs are in urban construction, providing highly irregular employment. In Chile, a fifth of Santiago's industrial workers are employed "in the notoriously occasional and unstable construction industry," according to economist Andrew Frank. In Central America, El Salvador is much envied for its industrial capability, but a recent survey conducted in five metropolitan areas shows that the service sector employs two and a half times as many persons as manufacturing

. . . a growing army of underemployed . . .

. . . the peasants began to move in force to the cities, and although their urban housing conditions were in many ways superior to those in rural areas, they suddenly became "deplorable." In fact, what had been invisible became visible, not only because the migrations were physically concentrated in the capital cities, but because the poor were suddenly under the very noses of the rich—so close, and in such numbers, that they could be not only seen but smelled.

and has been growing more rapidly over the past decade. Indeed, El Salvador's very industrial efficiency tends to discourage employment. Because of "the high ratio of technology to manpower," Pincus concludes, "the direct job-creating effects of this industrialization have been relatively small." The result is a growing army of underemployed, packed into urban slums and suburban shantytowns.

Even as judged by their own national censuses, two-thirds of all dwelling units in El Salvador and three-quarters of those in Honduras were substandard in the early sixties. In a typical poor neighborhood in Tegucigalpa, Cornell University researchers recently interviewed a representative sample of 450 household heads. They found that only 15 percent of them had been born in the city, that only 1 percent had been born in the *barrio* in which they were then living, and that a third had arrived in the *barrio* itself within the preceding 18 months. What kind of lives are they leading?

> Only three-quarters of the household heads had worked for all of the preceding six months, and not all of these worked full days.
>
> Forty percent of the households have no access to toilets or latrines.
>
> Women over 40 years of age have had an average of almost seven live births, but a quarter of those born will not live to adolescence.
>
> Although almost all declare themselves to be Catholics, only three-quarters of the couples declare themselves married.
>
> Half the adult women are illiterate. Of the balance only half read a newspaper.

What do the houses look like?

> The majority of barrio residents live in *cuarterias*, or rows of connected rooms. *Mesones de la calle* are single rows of such rooms that generally face the street; *mesones de los callejones* are arranged in double rows facing each other across a narrow alley, which may run the entire length of a block. Both types, together with other combinations of connected rooms scattered across back lots, are decidedly substandard. There is no owner-occupancy of this kind of housing. Constructed of wood or, less frequently, *bahareque,* and with earthen floors, they are generally windowless, with the door serving for both access and ventilation. An average of six persons and all functions of daily life are housed in the single room, sometimes with a small kitchen in the rear covered by the overhang of the tiled room. The *mesones de los callejones* are particularly oppressive, since the dirt alley between the buildings that face each other is barely wide enough for a person to walk through. The alley must serve as both a sewage and waste disposal area and as a long, narrow "courtyard" for as many as 120 or 150 persons.

Future prospects for housing in Honduras are grim. The ODECA report on Central American Housing set Honduras's housing deficit in 1965 at 263,000 units. Honduras's five year

> **The right to housing is a fundamental right in a democratic society.**
> PUNTA DEL ESTE DECLARATION

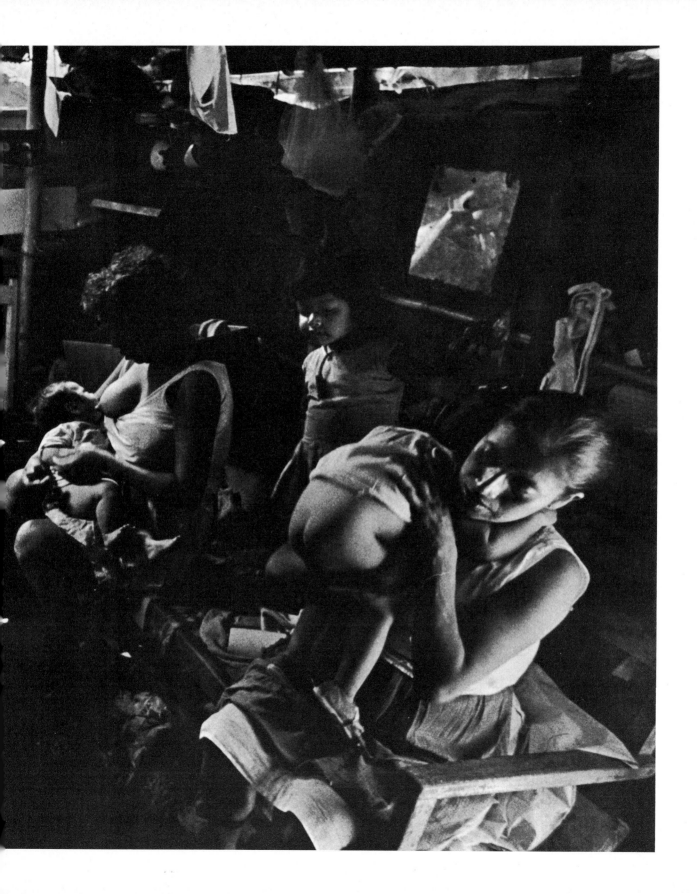

plan called for no more than 9,500 houses to be built between 1965 and 1969 in the public sector. *But by sheer population increase alone 64,000 new houses were needed in this period.* Thus the goal was set at only 15 percent of the need generated by population increase. Instead of diminishing, the huge deficit of houses increased during the term of the government's plan.

Most of these houses were too expensive for a substantial segment of the population in any event, and also too expensive for the government to consider on a scale commensurate with the need. An AID grant of over $1.5 million for housing in Honduras a few years ago resulted in a grand total of 253 homes. If this means the houses cost nearly $6,000 each, and if they were given to families at 5 percent interest, the annual interest alone would be over $300. In 1969, according to the Central Bank of Honduras, 45 percent of rural families earned less than $250 per year, and a quarter of the urban families earned less than $750. Such families can afford neither a $6,000 nor a $3,000 house, nor will the government ever be able to afford to give it to them.

In El Salvador, 3 percent of the government's budget is allocated to housing, but like Honduras, El Salvador is merely scratching the surface. The Instituto de Vivienda Urbana (IVU) has been building about 1,400 homes per year in recent years, but to keep up with population growth alone would have taken 7,000 units per year. As a 1968 IVU report put it:

> To deal with this problem the IVU was created in 1951, and by 1967 had built around 15,206 houses. . . .
>
> In the urban area, population increase and replacement alone require 28 new houses per day, but no more than 8 are being built. In 1968, 176,100 houses are needed for the urban area and in ten years an equal number will again probably be required just to cover the demand created by population growth. . . .
>
> 39 percent of the families cannot get housing because their incomes are less than $48 per month, which scarcely covers other necessary costs.

The report notes the IVU housing is directed at people whose income is between $48 and $240 per month, and estimates that half the urban population falls in this category. But a social worker who knows the urban barrios well told about one large IVU development from which most of the urban poor would be excluded:

> The IVU house costs $2,700. The rent is $10 per month, which means that 80 percent of the people that live in this zone could not live in an IVU house. Just remember $28 a month is the average income per family now. Before the war it was $40, but it has really gone down. Given that fact, is IVU going to build more houses? They will probably tell you, given the world credit situation, they can't do it.

PRIVATE ENTERPRISE HOUSING

There is, of course, private enterprise, but it seems to build only two kinds of housing—that which is far beyond the reach of the poor, and that which is expressly designed for the poor—substandard housing of high density and high rent. The squeeze on the poor begins with land:

> A lot of these landlords have land and nothing else. They don't have money and have trouble paying their taxes. So you divide up your land and sell lots; but to do it legally costs money— you have to put in streets, light posts, you have to have a topographical measurement, you have to leave space for a park and a school—so nobody does it legally. They just divide it up and sell it or rent it and you have illegal communities without water or light. [Community Organizer]

Private enterprise low-cost housing is a horizontal version of the tenement—the *mesón*. As defined by IVU, a *mesón* is "a kind of collective housing of permanent character, unhealthy, usually one room to a family, with common sanitary facilities located in a central patio. About 55,000 families live in *mesones*." As defined by El Salvador's Foundation for Minimum Housing the *mesón* is even less attractive. "In these dwellings, constructed of 10, 20, 30 and more rooms roughly 13 by 13 feet each, with common sanitary services, bad ventilation, etc., live a large number of people whose monthly income is between $36 and $48."

By packing many families into a small space and providing few utilities, the landlord can make a handsome profit from even the poorest populations. Thus, in Mesón Serpas, surveys conducted in 1969 and 1970 showed each of about 290 families paying 40 cents each per month for the use of a single water fountain—a total of $116 per month. Close to two-thirds of the salaries of the adults are under $40 per month and over a quarter earn less than $20 per month. Of special interest is the sewage problem. Of 220 families interviewed, only 42 had their own latrine and 26 had access to a neighbor's. *Thus about 70 percent have no access to a latrine.* The Department of Health survey notes with concern a decline in latrines, explaining that "the proprietors obliged the renters to dismantle their privies because they rent the land to build shacks (*champas*), not toilets. He who wants a toilet should pay for the land it occupies." A community of 1,500 people with only about fifty latrines generates some pretty strong smells—so strong that the middle-class neighborhoods around Las Serpas have been complaining. This may be one poor community that gets rapid help from government!

PHILANTHROPIC HOUSING PROGRAM

"The slums are hidden from the rich," an American working in El Salvador told us. "Most middle and upper class Salvadorans don't know they exist." One organization which is trying to make them visible is the Fundacion de Desarrolo y Vivienda Mínima, a private group organized in 1968 and dedicated to housing for the poor. Headed by Spanish Father Antonio Fernandez Ibañez (described by an acquaintance as "previously just a priest"), the Fundacion has received most of its contributions from wealthy Salvadorans seeking to do good without getting into controversial areas. It began innocently enough in 1968 with an attempt to restore thirty shacks in San Salvador destroyed by a flood. It has raised money from AID and from the government, and has financing promised for building over a thousand houses. Its directors argue that they are duplicating the efforts of neither the government nor private enterprise, since these cater only to families with monthly salaries in excess of $80. The Vivienda Minima house costs about $1,000 and caters to the family earning between $35 and $60 per month. What the cost of houses would be on a mass scale is not clear. "The Vivienda Mínima house," said one critic, "was subsidized by an incredible amount of voluntary labor, interest-free money, donated land, enthusiastic architects, and enthusiastic Peace Corps volunteers, a situation that could not be duplicated in mass. It remains to be seen what kind of houses the foundation will build and how cheap they will be."

In the meantime the Foundation is undergoing some interesting changes, symbolized by the self-conscious addition of the word "Development" to its title in 1970. Little by little it is being moved into the position of spokesman or pressure group for the urban poor, whose own recently developed organizations have neither money nor power. Thus, the foundation assisted the residents of Campamento 3 de Mayo in a struggle with their landowner (see p. 68) and has announced that "given the magnitude of the slum problem, we will have constantly to seek solutions to *the general problem* and not to particular problems." (Italics added.) While commendable, this raises a deep but generic problem for a private agency whose resources and policy making stem from the rich, but whose ideology and professional staff will inevitably pull in the direction of social reforms. The strain is already apparent to some observers. One of them analyzed the situation like this:

> Those to the farthest right in the foundation see it as a way of stopping communism or getting rid of the slums, which are a blight. Even the architects, who are liberal, are very afraid of the left, and the rich are just trembling that their land will be taken away.

Others in the foundation see housing not only as an end but as a means. They want it to take a creative and somewhat radical stance in the institutional life of this country. The community groups in this country are just so isolated they can't even begin to think about progress, much less revolution.

In order to gain more autonomy the foundation is now seeking assistance from foreign and international agencies. If successful, it will discover a whole new host of problems associated with such aid. And in the meantime, who is worrying about the increasing number of families earning less than $35 per month?

CAMPAMENTO THIRD OF MAY

In 1965 an earthquake occurred in San Salvador, dispossessing a large number of poor families, who were temporarily relocated on a piece of land belonging to the Dueñas family, one of the nation's largest landowners. In this way, El Campamento 3 de Mayo, named after the day of the earthquake, was born. While the loan was for an indefinite length of time. Dueñas took pains to insure that people would understand they were in transit. Private guards patrolled to make sure that cement floors and wooden structures would not be used in construction, that new settlers would be kept out, and that latrines not be dug. As time passed, however, more permanent structures were in fact built, new people slowly filtered in, and the residents dug their latrines under cover of darkness. After about five years a census showed a population of nearly 700, and the rumors were thick that Dueñas was preparing to kick the residents off the property. A Baptist Church project to help finance relocation to another spot fizzled, as did efforts to get the city mayor to secure another piece of land.

The residents then turned to Dueñas himself in an effort to get him to sell them the land at a low price. With the assistance of the Baptists and the Foundation for Minimum Housing, an interview with Dueñas was held, but he announced that he had promised the land to another institution. In response the community did an unprecedented thing—it petitioned the government to *expropriate* the land, and organized two protest marches to the National Legislative Assembly on February 17 and 19, 1971. Four days later the Campamento was mysteriously burned to the ground.

LA PRENSA GRAFICA

Incendio destruye campamento.—

RURAL HOUSING:
THE ROAD, THE RIVER, AND THE FENCE

While rural housing has always been inadequate, there has rarely been a problem of space to build a shack. But as land values rose, agriculture moved toward plantation crops, and the population increased, many peasants found it increasingly difficult to find a plot, not to mention holding a plot they thought they owned. One of El Salvador's biggest landowners, Juan Wright, told us that "El Salvador's basic problem is housing" and went on to tell us what was happening on his own plantations:

> I'd prefer that these people were off my property because all of this land could be producing. They live here and pay absolutely nothing. Some of these houses they built 10 or 15 years ago. They built on the lands of the river . . . land which could be irrigated. I've been building them houses farther in to limit the number; but we are negotiating for land outside the property. After all, if the owner says get off, they have to go. It's better that they own their own land, but credit is a problem. The Rural Land Parcels Program is a good one, if only the peasants weren't being stirred up by that priest.

In between the problems of city housing and housing in the open country is the growing problem in the towns. In El Salvador, the slums of Santa Tecla provide a frightening example of man's clumsiness at regulating his numbers, his physical location, and his social arrangements. Many of the poor came here because population growth and agricultural shifts forced them out of the country, but in a town surrounded by rich coffee plantations, there is no room to build a shack. The result in one instance is that the people have built on the edges of a tiny stream that runs through the plantation of a large landowner. Since this is choice

. . . the squatter, squeezed off the land by his own prolificity and the movement toward plantation crops, lives in the narrow belt between the public road and the landlord's fence.

coffee land, he has fenced in his property on each side of the stream, which is public property, leaving the stream and its narrow borders for houses. When we visited the conglomeration of seventy or eighty houses, the stream was almost dry and served as a passageway between the tightly packed houses. When we asked about latrines, one of the residents shrugged and pointed his head toward the fence.

Not a mile away we visited a similar group of houses, in this case settled on both sides of a narrow public road which ran through the coffee owner's property. Little by little the houses had closed in, until the "road" had become a path between the rows of houses and the two fences.

Indeed, throughout Honduras and El Salvador, one is very conscious of "fence housing." Characteristically, the squatter, squeezed off the land by his own prolificity and the movement toward plantation crops, lives in the narrow belt between the public road and the landlord's fence.

A HOUSE IN THE COUNTRY

Andrés Ramirez is a 37-year-old farmer in Southern Honduras. He reached the third grade in school, married at the age of 30, and now has four children. He works his father's land, rents some of his own, and does occasional day labor on plantations or other farms. He is a member of the community council, and after living several years with his mother-in-law, has sayed enough to start building his own house. A healthy, happy, rustic life? A few more details are needed.

The Land: Andrés's father had six manzanas of good farm-land—and six children. Each got one manzana to work, and the fertility on the land has dropped so noticeably that Andres knows it needs fertilizer, but cannot afford it.

The Crop: Andrés says he does not harvest enough to feed his family, but when there are emergencies like sickness he must sell the crop cheaply to buy medicine, then buy it back at a much higher price in order to eat.

The Job: In order to supplement the subsistence agriculture with a little cash, he works when he can as a day laborer. He earns 25 cents per day plus a meal. He has also migrated during the sugar-cutting or fruit-picking season and earned $1.50 per day, but was charged so much for food and subject to so many other difficulties and uncertainties that he will not do it again.

The Wife: Andrés's young wife has been very ill since her fourth child. On many days she cannot get up at all. Andrés sorely needs her help but fears she may not recover. A physician comes to the village only occasionally and on the one occasion he saw her diagnosed anemia and prescribed four injections and a specific wine. When asked why his wife had not delivered her baby at the hospital, he explained that "You need either money or a recommendation."

The House:

"Is this plot of land yours?"

"I have an agreement to buy it for $10 when I can."

"What about the house? I see you are building it."

"Well, I am beginning to make it if God wills and my wife's health improves."

"What does it cost to make it?"

"More or less 25 dollars, in wood and things."

"Where did you get the money?"

"I have been saving for two years in a savings club we have."

"How much do you put in at a time?"

"From 5 to 10 cents, depending on what is left over."

"Why don't you get a loan from the bank?"

"I own no land and my harvest is too small. I'm too poor for a loan."

UNION HOUSING

One type of nongovernmental housing is sponsored by the Honduras north-coast union *Sitraterco,* and is an example of moderately priced houses for relatively well paid, relatively secure, and relatively well-organized agricultural workers. Paid about $3 per day or about $70 per month and with opportunities for overtime, a banana cutter can manage to put aside a little for housing if his family is not too large. The union has borrowed money from AID for housing and has talked the fruit company into an arrangement whereby the worker pays half and the company half of the cost of a house in the $4,000-to-$5,000 range. This puts the rent or interest payment in a class which the worker can afford. But the banana worker works all year round, has a powerful and socially conscious union to back him and loan him money, and is paid handsomely by Honduran standards. Even so, it is not likely that many banana workers will ever live in this kind of housing. While the union has 9,000 members, it has built or is building less than 500 houses, and at the present time only the higher echelons of workers have moved in.

A NEW HOME OWNER

Juan Lopez married two years ago and now lives with his wife and two children in a *Sitraterco* house.

"For many years I lived in San Pedro and my dream was always to have my own house. I have worked for seven years for the company and for five of them lived on company property. In the strike of 1968 I was head of a strike committee and was imprisoned for seven days for a just cause. This made me think about where I was living and I moved here. I was paying $12.50 per month rent, always hoping I could save enough for my own house. Six days ago I moved into my own house and I'm happy, comfortable, and peaceful. I don't have the money to furnish it yet, but nobody gets to heaven in one jump.

"I never finished more than half of grade school. If I struggle all I can for my children maybe they won't make the university but they should make secondary. I have seen homes with many children, and by the grace of God they are always taken care of, but with great sacrifices, so I have decided it's better to have two . . .

"Once I pay off the house I would like to work at something else. Some of my friends have left the company and have their little shops, one a tailor, one a banker, and they live their own lives and depend on themselves, not on any company."

5
The School

Education is the one great hope held in common by all social classes in Latin America. The poor see it as the only bridge between their current misery and the future well-being of their children; the rich see it as a way of moderately civilizing the masses; international investors see it as a way of providing a skilled labor force and the basic human material of economic development; while national governments see it as the solution to everything from high birth rates to high rates of crime. Thus education is not only politically safe but universally demanded. Since schools and teachers are tangible and constant reminders of a government's efficiency and responsiveness to public opinion, the public in fact gets schools—at fantastic cost and incredibly little return.

There is no doubt about educational deficiencies in Central America. According to censuses in the early 1960s, every other adult in El Salvador and Honduras was illiterate and there were more children aged 7 to 13 out of school than in school. Spurred by the Alliance for Progress and a developmental ideology, these countries have made great efforts to expand the formal school system over the past decade. Indeed the relative magnitude of their effort is staggering: whereas the United States spends only 4 percent of its federal budget on education, El Salvador and Honduras spend about 23 percent. El Salvador carried out an especially ambitious school construction program in the mid-sixties, completing 2,400 primary school classrooms at a cost of $7.6 million. Thus by 1967 they could boast that 95 percent of the nation's children were enrolled in school at one time or another, and that at least two-thirds of the children of primary school age were actually attending school. A substantial return on a substantial investment but for one fact—*most of these children will leave school still illiterate.*

To comprehend this we must first understand that most of the nation's educational effort is directed at primary schooling. Two-thirds of the national educational budgets are expended on these six grades. How useful are six years of education? As expressed in an official document of El Salvador's Ministry of Education: "Primary school does not capacitate students in the skills necessary for economic development. . . . [The students who go no further than sixth grade] abandon school just at the time they can begin to absorb the knowledge and attitudes useful for economic development."

A study by the Economic Commission of Latin America was able to document the ineffectiveness of the few years of schooling. In a survey of lower-income males in Santiago, Chile, it was found that earning capacity did not increase with years of schooling until five or more years of education were attained. Similar

findings have been reported with respect to reproduction: women's fertility appears to decline significantly only after six years of education have been attained. The emphasis on primary school could to some extent be justified if it meant that children were *completing* primary school, but few do. In the United States there are about as many children in the sixth grade as there are in the first; but in Honduras there are seven times as many first- as sixth-graders. In El Salvador, for every 100 students in the first grade in 1967, 80 failed to graduate from the sixth.

Part of the reason is shortage of schools. Half the Honduran primary schools did not contain more than three grades in 1965, and the rural situation is much worse. Two-thirds of the rural schools in El Salvador had no more than three grades in 1967, and only 12 percent had all six grades. In order to pursue studies beyond the third grade the typical rural student has to attend an urban school; in fact, one out of every five students in urban schools is a rural student. But sending a rural child to an urban school may mean both effort and money. Few rural families have the latter, and most do not expend the former.

THE COUNTRY SCHOOL

But the availability of schools is only part of the problem. A closer look at the rural school situation in El Salvador shows that education consists essentially of one grade—the first. In 1967 half the pupils in rural schools were in the first grade and half of the first graders did not go on to the second grade. This was not because there was no second grade to go to; although one of every four rural schools had only one room, virtually all have a second grade. Of the rural first-graders who failed to go on to second grade, *about half were not promoted and a quarter left school before the end of the year.*

Between a quarter and a third of all first grade students have been failing to pass in recent years—a clear indication that the educational system does not meet the needs of rural children. Students average 8 years of age on entering first grade, and a third are aged nine or older. Doubtless the sudden introduction to the strange rituals of a highly formalized middle-class educational system is a traumatic experience for the children of many poor families, partially accounting for the fact that over one in ten first-graders leaves before the end of the year. Moreover, the seasonal nature of plantation crops—coffee, sugar, and cotton—results in the large-scale migration of families during the harvest—and a disruption in the children's education. A teacher put it this way:

> The father depends on temporary labor, and during the six months' harvest the children are in school, but afterwards they leave. Or in the rainy season, with good pasture and lots of milk, the hacienda may need five men, but in the summer three will be laid off.

THE CITY SCHOOL

While the absence of the higher grades of primary school is an important factor in the rural setting, 85 percent of El Salvador's urban schools contain all six grades. Nevertheless, the majority of students are found in the first and second grade, and over a third of the first-graders fail to go on to the second grade. As in the rural area, half of these are not promoted. In contrast to the rural area, however, virtually all of those promoted go on to the second grade. Most significant is the fact that close to *half of the urban children who fail to go on to the second grade drop out before the end of the first grade.* To find out why, we visited three schools in lower-income neighborhoods. In each school we found almost four times as many enrolled in the first as in the sixth grade. Although the children were from families often living in one-room shacks, the schools resembled modern schools every-where, the teachers well dressed and often elegantly coiffured, and the uniformed children looking more spick and span than North American children. Since shoes and uniforms cost money, we asked the principal whether they were obligatory. "We ask the boys to wear white shirts and blue pants, and the girls white blouses and blue skirts," she replied, "but we don't really require it." Misunderstanding the point of our question, she called two shoeless girls without uniforms to the front of the class and asked them why they had no uniforms. Highly embarrassed, the girls replied that their mothers could not afford to buy them.

There are other pressures on the children to purchase materials or to engage in activities which involve cash outlays. In the lower grades they must buy pencils and notebooks, and in the upper grades even more expensive materials. There are numerous social affairs, including beauty queen contests for each grade. The girl who "wins" must be dressed and coiffured appropriately for the ceremony. What seems like pennies to a middle-class teacher can be a terrifying financial burden for a family with an unemployed father, or with no father.

Again, just as migratory labor discourages school attendance in the rural area, the high mobility of the urban poor can disorganize the child's educational experience. A survey conducted by Cornell University in a Tegucigalpa neighborhood served by one of the schools we visited showed that a fifth of the families living there had moved into the neighborhood within the past six or seven months. Moreover, household heads had moved an average of three times within the city, and one in seven had moved five or more times.

There is also the problem of health among the urban poor. As one teacher put it, "Sometimes we have continual epidemics, and if the child misses a few weeks he doesn't want to come back." Malnutrition lowers the energy level of children, thus weakening

> **The public gets schools at fantastic cost and incredibly little return.**

their motivation and ability to learn. Unlike the rural family, the city family must pay cash for every piece of food it consumes. It is probable that urban families are more likely than rural ones to reduce or alter food consumption habits when economically pressed. With inadequate school feeding programs, the children are the most intense sufferers.

Perhaps most important of all in contributing to the school dropout rate is the need for cash on the part of the urban family. It is not generally recognized that under present conditions of rural labor surplus and land scarcity on the one hand, and urban cash needs on the other, that urban child labor may be more crucial to family income than rural child labor. The 1965 figures for Honduras show that more boys than girls were enrolled in elementary school in the villages, but more girls than boys in the more urbanized areas where there are more "jobs" for a small boy than for a small girl. Moreover, while there are 8 percent more boys than girls in the first grades of the nation's schools, there are over 10 percent more girls in the sixth grade. The deficit of boys begins in the fourth grade, when the average child would be 11 or 12—an ideal age for selling papers, guarding cars, shining shoes, and selling Chiclets. Competing among thousands in the city, the child can nevertheless bring in a few pennies a day—enough for a stick of firewood or a pot of coffee.

In one school the principal had followed up 25 children who had dropped out of school in 1969. Seven of the 25 had done so in order to go to work. A few examples taken from the principal's notebook give the flavor of these cases:

> Norma Angelica, fifth grade. Irregular attendance from the beginning of the year. Now a vendor in the market. She hardly remembers school and thinks only of what she's earning.
>
> José Manuel, third grade. The mother says they need him to work, and although we advised him to work harder, he said she had begged to be allowed to work, and now sells fruit in the street.
>
> José Manuel, third grade. The mother says they need him to help construct wooden beds.
>
> Wilfredo, third grade. Has to work assisting a shoemaker.

The precarious economic existence of the lower class family is frequently worsened by unstable marital relationships, which compel the mother to enlist the support of her children. "It's the rare child," said one teacher, "who lives with his mother and father. One child had to start selling lottery tickets to support his mother and other brothers and sisters because he is the oldest child." Many teachers complained of absenteeism during part of the day or part of the week, but feel they must permit it. As one of them put it, " 'Teacher,' they say, 'let me out this morning so I can sell tortillas.' 'Teacher, this afternoon I have to sell newspapers,' they say. So I let them go rather than have them lose the whole day."

The deficit of boys appears in the fourth grade when the average child would be eleven or twelve—an ideal age for selling papers, guarding cars, shining shoes, and selling chiclets.

Many of the problems described in connection with the urban dropout are illustrated in the history of Luis, a child who· had dropped out of the first grade.

Luis is a bright-appearing child of nine who dropped out in order to sell tamales in the street. He had 11 siblings, 6 of whom live with his father and 5, plus himself, with his mother. He says he can read a little and would like to learn more so he could earn as much as his brother—$10 per week. His mother had the following to say:

> He was in the first grade but I had to take him and his brothers out. It's too bad. They were good in school, but there were times when there was no breakfast and no lunch. And the clothes—if one had them the other didn't. Sometimes the social worker would give us milk, but she hasn't come for three months. I told her, "Look I'm not so interested in that—how about helping with school supplies, so I can keep the kids in school," and she said, "Well I can give you wheat and flour, but no notebooks. Maybe next year," she told me. You need notebooks, pencils and then morning, noon, and night it's 10 cents for this and 15 cents for that; that's why I can't take that school. You don't have enough for a cup of coffee, for a piece of firewood and the school wants money. I live for my children but where would I get $2.50 for supplies for this one alone? It's $2.50 for supplies in the first grade, $7.50 in the fourth grade and $15.00 for the sixth grade!

> My kids cry to go to school, but with no breakfast, I had one who fainted. Better they don't go at all. They used to give them a cup of milk, but not now. The weak ones can't study without eating.

> My hope is that the big ones will grow up soon and help me with the little ones.

POPULATION, POVERTY, AND SCHOOLS

It is difficult to see how countries like Honduras and El Salvador can spend a higher proportion of their budgets on education; indeed it would be very helpful to the solution of other national problems if they spent *less*. The latter course would be possible only if the rate of population growth fell markedly or if the educational system were more effective. Just keeping up with future population increase will be a major task. In El Salvador, where there were about 500,000 children aged 7 to 12 in 1967, there will be 720,000 in 1976—an increase of over 200,000. In what it calls a "program of massive construction between 1962 and 1967," the Ministry of Education added 2,364 classrooms with a capacity of roughly 95,000 students. Indeed, the ministry noted ruefully that in the rural area "the new schoolrooms built between 1963 and 1967 had a capacity of 30,000 students, but rural enrollment increased by 60,000." Naturally, the ministry now has bigger and better plans for the next five-year period, when they hope to build another 3,000 classrooms, with help from international agencies and community "self-help" building

programs. Since each classroom costs over $3,000 to build, and since each student costs nearly $40 per year, the help will have to be of significant proportions.

But assuming that the supply of new teachers and schools can outrace population growth, the question remains as to whether a real improvement in educational levels will be effected, and whether more of the traditional primary school training will do much for the poor.

Certainly their poverty, mobility, and family disorganization will continue to keep many from taking advantage of whatever new schools may be built. It was Luis's mother who, speaking of the crowded public schools of Tegucigalpa, said, "Those schools are not for the poor. They're for the rich."

There are also dangerous psychological risks to be taken in an educational scheme which ejects so many of its aspirants. As Father Ivan Illich puts it, "School inevitably gives individuals who attend it and then drop out, as well as those who don't make it at all, a rationale for their own inferiority."

Even these risks would be worth taking if the price was reasonable, but it may be true, as suggested by Illich, that "to buy the schooling hoax is to purchase a ticket for the back seat in a bus headed nowhere." The ticket, as we have seen, is not cheap.

In the rural area the new schoolrooms built between 1963 and 1967 had a capacity of 30,000 students but rural enrollment increased by 60,000.

For every hundred students entering the first grade ninety will fail to graduate from the sixth.

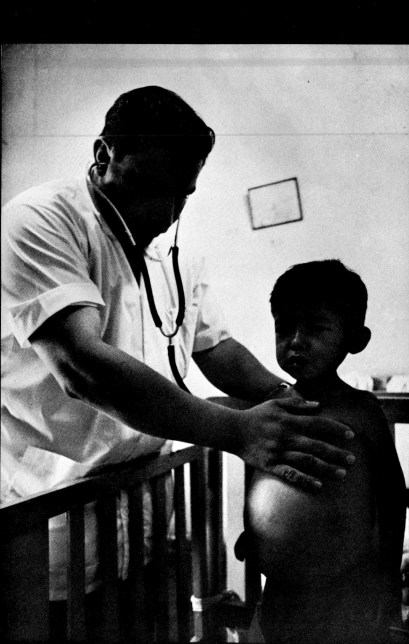

One indication of a nation's probable health is the proportion of physicians in its population. This standard alone indicates a health problem in Central America—its six nations have fewer physicians than the state of Tennessee. The gap in medical personnel between Europe and America on the one hand, and Central American republics on the other is shown in Table C.

It is bad enough to have so few physicians; what is much worse is that the doctors huddle together in a few cities with the same concern for private patients and specialization that characterizes the physician on Park Avenue.

The first important fact about Honduran physicians is that one in every ten of them is not there. Of the 675 doctors registered in the Medical Association, 74 are out of the country—an indication of the brain drain and the pursuit of exotic specialties. Next, of those who are in Honduras, over two-thirds are in Tegucigalpa, San Pedro Sula, and La Ceiba, cities which account for only 16 percent of the population. In Honduras's eight poorest departments, which contain 550,000 people—over a fifth of the population—there are exactly 28 physicians, half of whom are young interns putting in their government service.

Part of the reason for the maldistribution of doctors is the classical orientation of the medical profession toward specialization and the economics of private practice. Dr. Dominguez, one of a handful of female physicians in Honduras, said, "Yes I want to practice in a big city, or abroad. To work in a village you don't need to specialize. If you have a specialty you forget it within a year in a village." Of course the reason the specialty is forgotten in the village is not only the lack of expensive equipment and lab facilities but the fact that it is not *needed*, certainly not when compared with the needs stemming from common infectious diseases. While the acute needs are for the prevention and treatment of infectious diseases among the rural and urban poor, preventive medicine has little prestige. "The majority of medical students wants to cure, not prevent, disease," says Dr. Dominguez. "Everybody approves of preventive medicine but nobody wants to practice it."

A Salvadoran physician, Dr. José Manuel Gavidia, puts it more bluntly: "The majority of medical students regards preventive medicine as a waste of time. Most study medicine intent only on a good economic future and with a false idea of the role of the physician in a society such as ours. They dream of a lush clinic with a rich clientele in a romantic setting they have seen in foreign movies or television."

A university professor dissected his medical school's élitist approach to medicine: "Our university has been producing doctors to cure the ills of the upper classes. The very curriculum is devoted to this, so that few doctors ever get to a village. When he

6
Health

Table C			
Medical Personnel per 100,000 Population, 1965			
	Physicians	Dentists	Nurses
Switzerland	141	39	278
Spain	126	10	75
Greece	141	41	63
USSR	210	30	340
Poland	126	37	229
Yugoslavia	83	18	89
USA, New England states	168	53	470
USA, east-south-central states	89	31	165
El Salvador	22	6	24
Honduras	16	5	8

is sent there by the government, he is totally frustrated because he hasn't been trained to take care of the needs of a poor population."

In Honduras one professor was attempting to convince the medical school to create a new field for medical auxiliaries, men and women with primary school teaching certificates who would be given three additional years of training in medicine, cooperatives, agriculture, and community development. They would work in the small villages in the employ of the government. Not surprisingly, he encountered stiff opposition from the medical profession, and a polite indifference from the international agencies.

THE DOCTOR

Having read press reports of a severe epidemic of dysentery in the department of Chalatenango, El Salvador, we were anxious to visit the hospital there. Chalatenango is a heavily populated, arid, and especially poor zone bordering Honduras, and we thought it might give us a glimpse of the nutrition problem in a rural area. A medical report on the region had described it as "wild and ill-suited to much agriculture. The population which shows up at the clinics evidences severe malnutrition of all kinds, and intestinal parasitism is widespread."

The 48-bed Chalatenango hospital serves a population of 163,000. Like many Latin American hospitals, its occupancy rate exceeds 100 percent because there is often more than one person

> Hospital occupancy rates exceed 100 percent because there are often more than one person per bed.

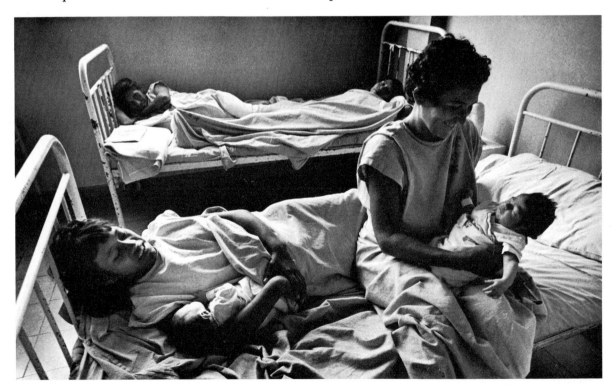

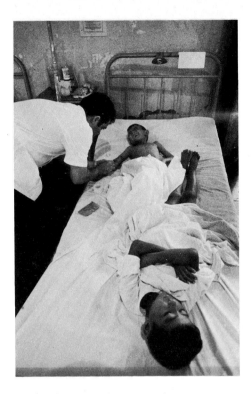

per bed. The 6 beds in the maternity ward and the 12 cribs in pediatrics most frequently have more than one occupant, and because of the dysentery epidemic the latter ward was especially full. We picked our way around bloody diapers on the floors, being especially careful not to disturb the flies. Our attention was caught by a child who kept trying to stand in his crib, and, apparently too weak, kept falling down and crying in dismay. We commented to the nurse on his apparent malnutrition and she cheerfully lifted him out for a picture. "Most of them here are undernourished," she said, "and only partly because of the dysentery. Their parents don't even know they're undernourished; some of them think these big stomachs mean the child is healthy. The main cause of their malnutrition is the ignorance of their parents, who sell the best food they grow instead of giving it to the children."

We doubted the matter was so simple and recalled the words of Dr. Gavidia: "If we deigned to be interested in a malnutrition case we tended to attribute it to simple neglect or ignorance, which was beyond our responsibility to treat." Certainly only acute dysentery and the grossest symptoms of malnutrition were being treated here during the child's few days in the hospital. How soon would it be before they would be back, hungrier and sicker?

We turned to another child with swollen legs and genitalia and asked the doctor if he knew the case. "Not really," he said. "Third degree malnutrition case—underweight by over 40 percent. Because of the tremendous pressure of cases we can't really treat the basic causes. Anyway, the doctor can't solve this problem; it takes the economist, the industrialist, the lawyer. It's true that education is part of it—there are women who sell their hens' eggs rather than feed them to the child, then use the money to buy him a strawberry colored soft drink because they think it will fortify his blood. But basic production of foodstuffs has to be improved, too. It's a complex problem, not a simple one."

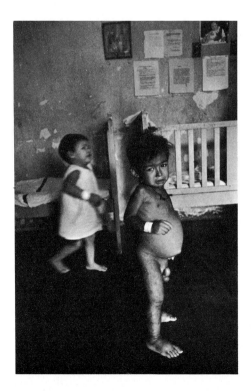

We thought so too, and urged Dr. Chinchilla, three years out of medical school, to tell us more about the problems of the demands on his tiny hospital. "The demand is increasing fast," he replied, "not only because of population increase, but because recent governments have put in roads and public transportation into the once remote sections. They did it to facilitate the transport of agricultural goods, but it's had the effect of bringing in the sick to the hospital. The number of sick is the same, but the doctor sees more of them now. They used to die and who knew about it? Three years ago this child would never have come here because there was no road and no bus."

"But with that growing demand and a region of 163,000 people to serve how can you make do with 48 beds?" we asked.

"We're building a new hospital," he replied proudly, "and it will have a *hundred* beds."

NUTRITION

In southern Honduras Rodney C. Stares has recently done a careful study of the economy of the small farmer. His preliminary analysis shows a tight and vicious circle of population increase, malnutrition, economic exploitation and low productivity. Put together, they spell increasing poverty for the encircled victims.

What has happened has been twofold: first, a slow but significant reduction in mortality rates, especially among children, largely as a result of preventive medicine programs, better knowledge, increased malaria control and availability of pills and medicines; secondly, a gradual rise . . . in consumption demand both from the necessity to feed the increased numbers of children surviving and the increased desire to buy new consumer "necessities." [This has been accompanied by] decreased ability to produce more [because of] the virtual arrival at the land frontier and the sharply diminishing returns of continually using the existing land in the traditional way. When inheritance patterns and traditional techniques are taken together with the erosive forces of the environment, soil fertility is likely to decrease rapidly. . . .

With the erosion of reserves the *campesino* can't afford to store his crop through to the end of the season when grain is scarce but has to sell it at harvest time when the price is at its lowest. Later, when his small reserves of corn are exhausted, he has to buy his corn back again at very high prices. . . . Gradually the *campesino* moves to a position in which he sells his crop before the harvest to the buyer or money lender at a considerable discount, often as high as 50 percent. Often when the buyer is a store owner the *campesino* will be given credit to buy in the store; hence, the store man makes a double profit, one on his grain purchase and secondly on the goods sold. . . .

In part, the deficit is closed by reducing the nutritional quality of family diets and hence the cost of the subsistence minimum. The younger children especially in the most affected families will increasingly show the various manifestations of malnutrition and debility which will in their turn produce an increased expenditure on pills and medicines. . . .

One of the commonest responses to the periodic family crises is the sale of farm animals, especially pigs and chickens. These relatively protein-rich foods can usually command a high price in the local markets, and with the proceeds *campesinos* can often buy sufficient corn to feed the family for perhaps several weeks, or afford relatively expensive medicines or treatments. It is therefore at this point that the vicious circle of nutritional deficiency and debility act to reduce the *campesino*'s future capacity to meet economic challenges.

Usually the first few children in the family will receive the benefits of the young healthy mother's food supply during their prenatal stage and be fed during their critical early years a wider range of nutritive foods. Gradually, however, to feed the increasing numbers of children and to buy the new consumer goods, the most nutritionally valuable foods are sold to buy basic staples. With the sale of larger percentages of family vegetables, egg, milk, cheese, and fruit production, the mother's

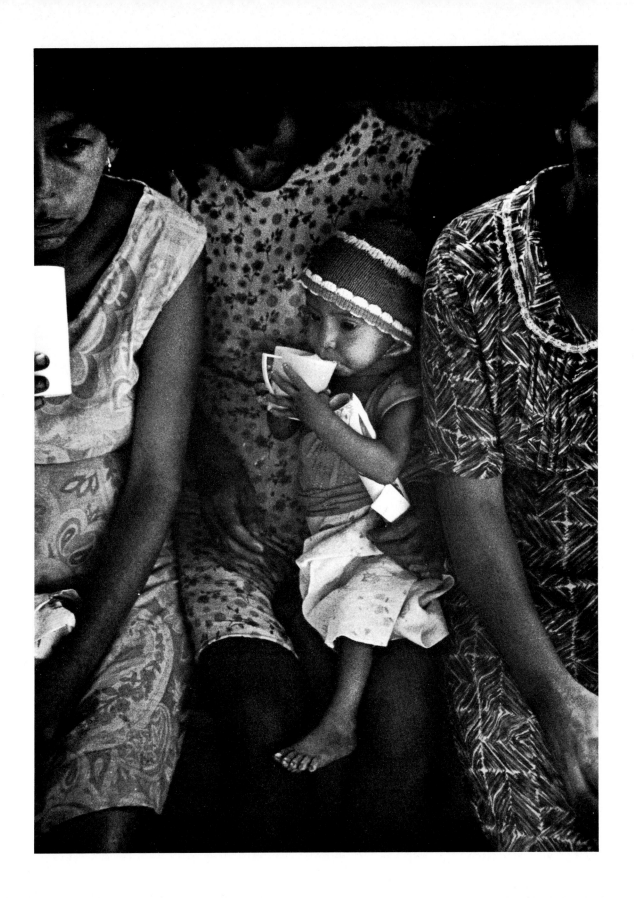

strength and vitality is declining, as is the nutritional content of the baby's food. . . .

In the process of population growth the quality of the surviving children is being reduced. . . .

Currently, women giving birth to children in the southern region have both blood cell counts 40 percent below normal and an average hemoglobin of 40 percent below the minimum desirable levels for childbirth. Taken together, these two statistics imply that the oxygen-carrying power of the average *campesino* mother's blood is at childbirth some 60 percent below desired levels. . . .

Such commonly noted Central American characteristics as laziness and lack of energy are hence usually the result of deficient infantile nutritional intakes; a biological heritage of low-protein and low-vitamin diets has resulted in a lowering of maximum energy outputs.

The six Central American nations have fewer physicians than the state of Tennessee.

THE ABORTION

In the maternity hospital of San Salvador one out of every five women is getting rid of a baby rather than having one. Virtually all these women arrive with incomplete abortions, many of them hemorrhaging and requiring emergency treatment and blood transfusions. The number has increased from about 2,000 per year in the mid-fifties to 3,000 per year in the late sixties, severely taxing the capacity of a hospital essentially designed for normal hospital deliveries. About a dozen of these women die every year; the others, after curettage and a few days' rest, are released to conceive again.

Since abortion is a criminal offense, it is not surprising that few women admit that the abortion was induced, but it is of interest that the hospital classifies no more than a third of them as "spontaneous." On the other hand, few are prosecuted. In 1965, for example, only seven persons in the entire nation were indicted, and only one convicted.

Dr. Madrigal of the maternity hospital staff gave us a succinct explanation of the technology, economics, and politics of abortion:

> The method they use in 90 percent of the cases is *la sonda*, a rubber instrument. Then they use all sorts of metallic instruments like nails or umbrellas. Once I had a patient come in with a pen still in the cervix. Lately they use vaginal douches of half water and sulphuric acid, I think. I can tell most of the time if they've used the *sonda* because of the lesions in the cervix. Of course they put the *sonda* in but they don't curettage the patient, so we have to do that.

> An abortion done by a doctor would cost them from $80 to $100. The abortionist only charges $4, and then the patient comes here to get the job finished. It's cheaper that way, and we do the best job! And the abortionist tells the patient what to say and what not to say. They tell the patient, "Don't say that you know me, don't say I live in this city."

Despite Dr. Madrigal's warning, we worked with a social worker and managed to get one patient to admit the identity of her abortionist. Rosa Perez is a 34-year-old woman on her fifth pregnancy, with two living children, the youngest five years old. Since she works as a live-in maid, the children live with her mother, and she sees her common-law husband every eight days. She claims she went to a practical nurse she had heard about from a friend, and was not sure she was pregnant. The nurse told her she was not pregnant but had "dangerous coagulants which could form tumors and should be treated. She put me in a big chair and stuck in some pincers, like scissors. When I saw blood she said, 'If you bleed a lot, buy some ergotrate pills at the drug store.'" She paid eight dollars, and after experiencing a variety of symptoms came to the hospital where she "discovered" she had had an abortion.

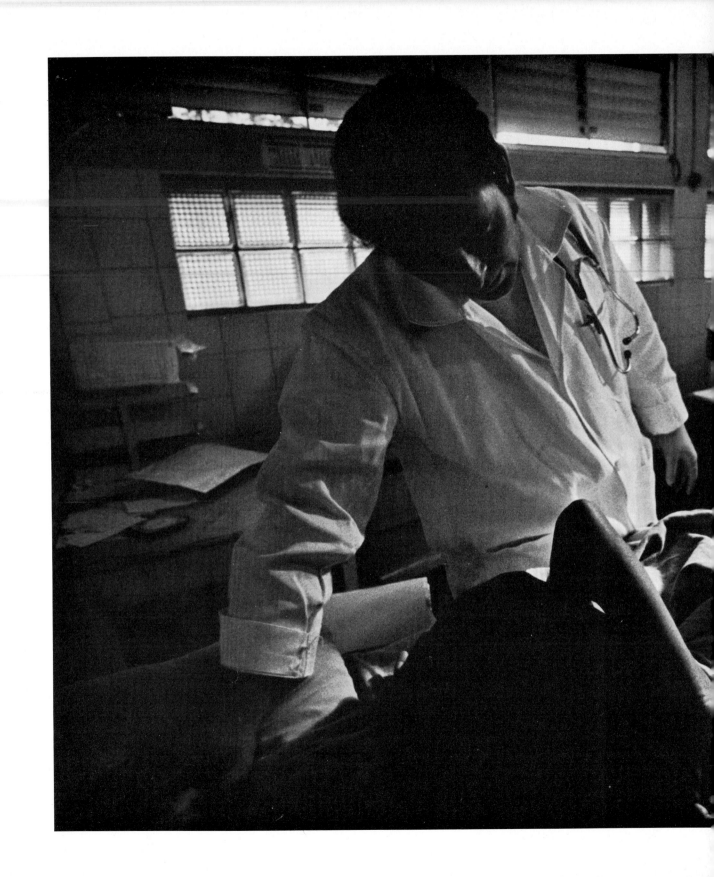

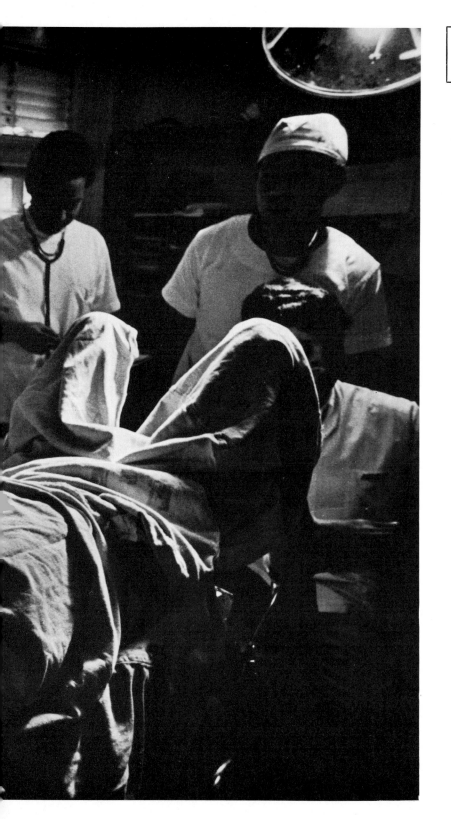

I have seen patients die refusing to
tell who did the abortion.

DR. DOMINGUEZ

The social worker then located the abortionist, a 77-year-old almost illiterate midwife, blind in one eye, and with partial vision in the other. Living in conditions described by the social worker as "dirty and frightening," she had a "simulated gynecological chair, a douche bag on the wall, and a small adjoining room where she probably keeps her tools." In the course of a lengthy interview she repeatedly denied ever performing an abortion, but had some interesting comments to make about what might be her principal current threat—the intrauterine device: "Women are putting in those 'spirals' to keep from having children. A woman came to me with a terrible pain and strong hemorrhaging. I examined her and found that little ring inside which I'd never seen. I've got it right here in a can! They get pregnant anyway with that thing in. The child is born with it in his stomach, or on the top of its head. Even nurses tell me that!"

Not all cases employ such professionals. Teresa is a 24-year-old girl who works in a beauty parlor. After 15 weeks of pregnancy she inserted a *sonda* herself, left it in for 24 hours, hemorrhaged for two days and then came to the hospital. She has a three-year-old child, a product of a relationship with a married salesman who left her when the child was one year old. She took various steps to get him to support the child: "I went to court a year and a half ago. He claimed he didn't know me, much less have a child by me. Later I got very sick and got him to come to my house. We talked, and to keep me quiet he said he would send me money, but he never has. I think the court is no good for women. They favor the men."

A year ago she began seeing a university student, and was soon found out by his fiancée and his parents. When she became pregnant he told her it was up to her to decide if she wanted to have the child or not, and left her. "I don't earn much," she said. "I couldn't have another child. I had heard about the *sonda* and got someone to buy one for me. It was very dangerous, but . . ."

These cases illustrate how the social and economic circumstances can force the woman to an act which is painful, dangerous, against her own moral standards, and often expensive—and is nevertheless the lesser of two evils. To make the having of a child such an evil is the first symptom of a sick society; the second is giving such women better access to dangerous remedial techniques than to harmless preventive ones. The "joke" is on the society, of course, which must pay the bill. Aside from the costs in health and well-being, there are also some direct ones: at the maternity hospital, each abortion case costs the state just under $75. Each year the hospital spends over $200,000 on abortion cases, a figure which is over half its entire annual budget.

In the Maternity Hospital one out of every five women is getting rid of a baby rather than having one.

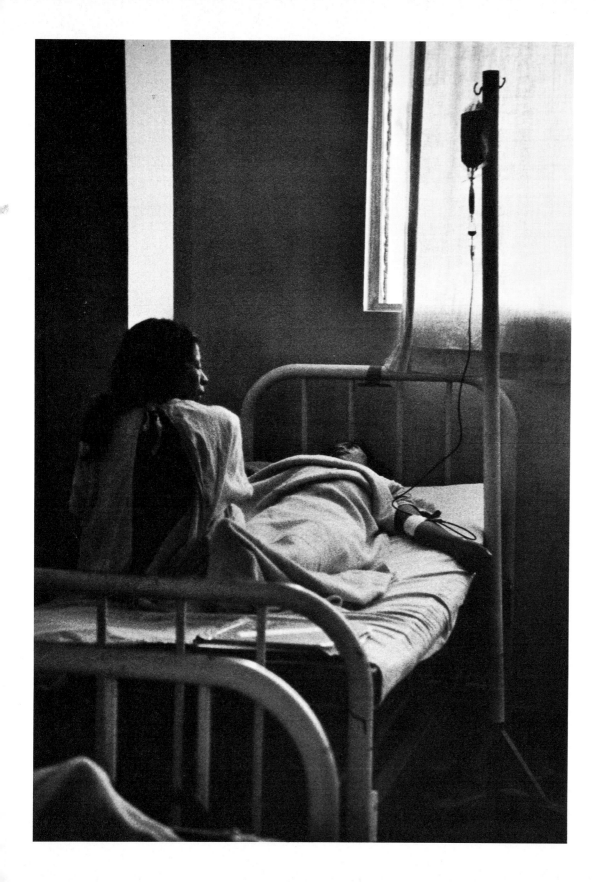

7
Working Women

Statistics on Latin American cities show a surprising number of employed women, giving the impression of a relatively favorable state of affairs for the female. The fact is that the armies of working women in the cities are in highly depressed occupations—vendors in the marketplace and domestic servants in the homes of the middle and upper classes. An unrecorded but sizable number enter prostitution.

In late 1970 the Salvadoran newspapers were full of discussions of what the mayor of San Salvador described as "our sad social reality, the 7,000 ambulatory market women in the capital city." The mayor blamed both the population explosion and rural-to-urban migration, admitting that new central markets under construction will do little to solve the problem. A group of indignant middle-class women had petitioned the mayor to turn back the "invasion of the streets" by the market women, reminding him that "there are other, more worthy, sources of employment for such women, like domestic service."

As a result of a surfeit of women seeking employment, their low levels of preparation, and a family system which puts the burden of unplanned procreation on the women, there are hordes of "employed" women in the cities struggling to survive. Many of them, abandoned after having a child or two, are striving for the survival of their children. To illuminate their struggle, we have chosen representatives of the three occupations mentioned above —a maid, a prostitute, and a street vendor.

A LIVE-IN MAID

Marta is a 26-year-old country girl who dropped out of the first grade after six months. She lives at the back of an upper-class home in a tiny room next to the tubs used for washing clothes. The room is just large enough for the cot and small table with which it is furnished. A second person could only sit on the cot, but this is not a problem since she is not allowed to have visitors. We asked her mistress about the problems of live-in maids and she told us the following:

> Actually I do most of the work, but I want it that way because they live like pigs in their homes, and here I teach them how to keep their room—even to put flowers in it. Where they come from they live 12 in a room; here I don't have more than two in that room.
>
> They have Sundays completely free. They like to go out with their little boyfriends. They rarely marry, just go out with the boys, have children; then the men leave them and they start all over.
>
> I pay $17.50 a month, and once you get them trained and somebody offers them 50 cents more they leave you.

Not surprisingly, Marta's point of view is somewhat different. Six months ago she left her country home and still longs for it.

"Everything in the city costs money," she notes, reflecting that without cash not even firewood or beans can be obtained. "If you don't have money you don't eat," she says; indeed, it is only for money that she came to work in the first place:

"How do you like working here? You get Sundays off?"

"No, just Sunday afternoons from three to seven. I go with my cousin to [a suburb] and we walk around and have an ice cream. During the week I can't speak to anyone. If my girl friends come asking for me she tells them I'm not here, or that I'm busy. Sometimes, I get angry—it could be about my family —but I don't say anything, even if I'm burning inside."

"Why did you leave the country?"

"I lived with my husband for five years and had five children, Three died. Then he began seeing another woman and when we had the last child he said it wasn't his. But they were all his— he just wanted to live with her. So he left me two years ago, and having the two children, I had to do something to live. We didn't even have a house to live in. So I decided to come here and save enough to buy a piece of land back home and build a house; so that if I die tomorrow my children won't just be help-less. That was the idea I had, so I left the children with my mother and got this job, and if God only helps me . . ."

"Do you think you will make it?"

"Well, I have nothing now. I get $15 a month. She told you $17.50!? The land will cost $50, and I haven't saved anything because I had to send clothes and things to the children. But between now and December . . ."

"Then what? How would you support the children back there?"

"Well, you always have a few chickens, and you find odd jobs now and then, you live poor but you can make out. God gives you life . . ."

A YOUNG BUSINESS WOMAN

Norma Maria had just had her 17th birthday when we inter-viewed her at the detention center. Though a bit on the hard side, she impressed us as a bright and capable girl. Her psychological report indicated normal intelligence and superior numerical abil-ity. It also indicated she had twice been treated for venereal disease, had first been brought to the juvenile court at age 15 and again at 16, on both occasions for vagrancy and prostitution. Other records show her to be a girl of unusual administrative and entrepreneurial ability. At age 15 or 16 she had successfully introduced several other girls into prostitution, managed them and their money, and kept them in line by guile, threats, blows, and gifts. We will never know how her talents became channeled in this particular direction, but her educational and family back-ground give some interesting leads:

Age	School Grade	Age	School Grade	Age	School Grade
7	First	10	Second	13	Third
8	Second	11	Third	14	Fourth
9	Second	12	Third	15	Fourth

These data may reveal more about the school system than about the student; but for a girl of normal intelligence and great drive to spend nine years to achieve the fourth grade must have required great forebearance, and must have provoked enormous frustration. This is as much as we know of her schooling, but the reports contain more information about her parents.

Father: A man of violent character. . . . Reports he has known of Norma Maria's existence for only three years. Shortly after her birth a woman representing the mother came to announce Norma Maria's death. He was asked for money for the child's funeral, and he sent $25 to her mother. In any event he did not believe the child was his since the mother was having relations with others at the time. Now he gives the child money occasionally but would not consider custody since her bad habits would disturb the harmony of his home.

Mother: An illiterate woman, she has used various methods of disciplining Norma but without results. Her son blames the mother for Norma's conduct, saying she set a bad example by her marital infidelity, though she was not a prostitute. He says Norma always threw it up at her that she had children by other men, and he could not tolerate this lack of respect.

Norma Maria's own version:

My mother had 18 children. Nine of them died. There were three fathers—well, four in all, counting the one she married. First mama got together with the father of my brother Juan; from there she got together with my father; from there a Salvadoran; and from there she got together with the one she married, and kept having children. But now she lives alone with three children.

My father doesn't love me. He told me in a letter my mother had been a whore and that I was just like her.

My mother is always beating me. She doesn't beat you like other people, she grabs machetes or anything. She would hit me when I burned something I was ironing, or if I let the tortillas burn: And if she ever bought me anything she was always throwing it up at me. So I said better I become a lost woman, I couldn't take it.

So I don't recognize mother or father. I have neither one. Look, not even shoes do they bring me!

What will happen to this spirited girl? None of her relatives wants her, and the social workers' report will surely keep her confined for some time. "She has no sense of guilt for perverting minors by force," it says, "and it would be therefore dangerous to free her." In addition to having her interned at an "educational center" and giving her a course in dressmaking, three recommendations were made: (1) weekly psychological treatment; (2) social work to teach her family "its responsibility, especially concerning human values;" and (3) social work which would give Norma Maria "human values and a new philosophy of life."

All these recommendations are directed at the symptoms, rather than the causes, and are efforts to adjust the individual and the family to a distorted social situation, which is the real source of the problems. In any event there is little likelihood that such measures will have any effect. We visited the educational center where Norma Maria will be sent, and we predict she will learn more than dressmaking.

THE STREET VENDOR

Maria Cristina is a 31-year-old working mother. She had her first child at 14 years of age, and has had six more, two of whom have died. With no husband and now with three children between the ages of two and ten to support, life is not easy, but she survives by helping a street vendor sell shoes. Since he has only a dozen pairs or so to sell, he often fails to have the proper pair to suit the customer's taste, size, or pocketbook. In this case, Maria runs to other vendors around the market, seeking the appropriate pair of shoes. If she finds the right ones she earns a commission of four or five cents.

Since there are not many customers per day, Maria could not keep up the payments of $10 per month on a rented room. After falling a year behind in her payments she decided to leave, and two years ago, then with five children, took up residence on the street. A small platform used in the day for selling vegetables is her floor, and by a clever arrangement of boards and a sheet of plastic she assembles a dormitory box on the sidewalk for her family each night. Maria has a large club to discourage drunks, especially from approaching her five-year-old girl.

Even rent-free, however, she found it difficult to support five children, and soon sold or gave away her 13-year-old girl to a Nicaraguan woman who will probably train her as a prostitute.

Since her income is uncertain from day to day, so is food, and the children have had to discipline their minds and stomachs to the nutritional irregularity. Maria speaks with pride of their stoicism and stamina.

> The children are plump because they can stand to be hungry. My children don't ask for food if I haven't sold anything during the day. They don't bother me with "Mama, I'm hungry, mama, I'm hungry." Of course, when meal time comes they begin to come around and the little girl says, "Are we going to eat, mama?"
> "No," I say.
> "Why not?"
> "I have no money today."
> Then later, she says to me, "Mama, if there's nothing today, then we're not going to eat."
> "That's right."
> "Oh, well, then I'm not going to ask any more."
> They are good children. They accept it.

A small platform used in the day for selling vegetables is her floor, and by a clever arrangement of boards and a sheet of plastic she assembles a dormitory box on the sidewalk for her family each night.

Illiterate herself, Maria decided to send the 10-year-old boy to school last year. She bought him a colored pencil and writing pads, but after the first day he came back without them. He soon developed a large boil "from all that reading and writing." The other children began to make fun of him and beat him. He came home crying one day and announced that they would kill him, and refused to go back unless his mother took him. She refused. He had lasted one month in the first grade at 10 years of age. Now he spends his time, as Maria puts it, "playing around the street, sliding on a piece of cardboard."

A month ago, a tragedy jarred Maria's life. Struck in the leg by a truck, she left her children for the day to go to the hospital. When she returned, her favorite child, a three-year-old boy, was missing. She believes he was stolen and lives in continual anxiety and hope. When we left her in November, she was praying that God would return him for Christmas. She also allowed herself a rare thought about the future. "Who knows when we will leave this place," she said. "When they grow up and can work, I suppose. Once you're old, it's hard to find work." But she soon brightened and showed us her infected leg. "See," she said, "it's drying."

THE ABANDONED CHILD

In the cases we have just described the illegitimate children were all cared for, with varying degrees of success, by the mother. But in many cases the situation is intolerable for the mother and the child is abandoned. Abandonment seems to be increasing, if newspaper attention to the problem is any gauge of its frequency, and self-righteous rhetoric about the need for "responsible parenthood" abounds. "Where are the parents of these children?" El Salvador's *Prensa Gráfica* asks piously. "Their nearly animal drive for procreation dominates their instincts." In fact, such animal drives are equally present at all levels of society, but the middle classes possess the economic resources to form more permanent unions while enjoying less permanent ones in which reproduction is regulated by modern technology. It is both gratifying and harmless for the middle classes to insist on more "education in family responsibility for the lower classes," when what they really need are *jobs*. A wise coffee grower analyzed the situation perfectly: "In the poorer classes, it's not that the father is irresponsible," he told us, "but that he isn't earning enough to live on; how can he be responsible without income?"

> **Where are the parents of these children?**
> PRENSA GRÁFICA

Given the facts of migratory and seasonal labor, high rates of unemployment, and income insecurity, it does not seem surprising that marital ties are loose; and in the light of ignorance and inadequate access to contraception, progeny are a frequent result. The thing to wonder at is the devotion of the mothers who struggle as street vendors and maids to provide for their children. But there are many less fortunate, who are abandoned by their mothers.

We located one person who has devoted her life to the problem of homeless children, and who is sensitive to its social and economic roots. Sister Maria Rosa is a nun who left the traditional activities of her order to found an impressive institution for homeless children in Honduras. Modeled on Boys Town, it now cares for over 400 children. It required remarkable persistence, courage, and ability for a woman to create such an institution in Honduras. We asked Sister Maria Rosa why she did it.

> The other nuns thought I was crazy and would soon come back. They thought I was looking for a man, they thought all sorts of things. But I had to do it. I got the idea at age 11 when I found out *I* was an orphan. I wanted other children to have as good a home as I had. But it took me 20 years with the order to get permission to do what I wanted to do.

> I started with the children who were in prisons with their fathers. If the father goes to jail the mother must work, and she

> **There are mothers who out of pure desperation to feed the child just leave it on the street.**
>
> SISTER MARIA ROSA

would bring the children to the prison. We had six-year-olds already used by men. Others had been born and raised in the prison. Now I have an arrangement with the prison. They send these cases here.

Forty percent of our children here are abandoned. Some are left at the hospital, some in the street. Some people will leave the child with a neighbor saying, "Mind the child for a minute, I'll be right back," and never return.

In most of our cases the father is unknown. The mother is alone with the child. She gets sick, or she dies and there is no one to care for the child. Here in Honduras if the woman has one or two children she can't work. Nobody wants to give her work with two children, and they won't rent her a house because they know she won't pay. These people wander the streets and sleep wherever the night overtakes them. There are mothers who out of pure desperation at not being able to feed the child just leave it on the street.

In the light of her emphasis on the helplessness of women, we wondered how Sister Maria Rosa would feel about family planning. While it could not solve the basic problem, it would at least alleviate the consequences. But in this respect Sister Maria Rosa was little different from many Honduran leaders. Her answer to our question was almost curt:

photo by J. Mayone Stycos

Honduras doesn't have enough people. Honduras can have many million more. I don't believe in family planning. That money should be used for education and development.

New Hopes for Agriculture

8
The New
Peasant

Small farmers in Latin America bear little resemblance to those in Europe or North America. As Wagley describes them, "they are generally poor, illiterate, in poor health, out of touch with the modern trends of their nation, and looked down upon as rustics by the town and city people." Describing the small farmer of southern Honduras, Rodney Stares writes: "Even today it is still possible to encounter *campesinos* who have probably never been more than ten miles away from the town in which they were born." In spite of this picture of the unchanging rustic, a new breed has been emerging in the past decade. Still poor and attached to the soil, the peasant is rapidly developing a social and political consciousness, is becoming angry, and is organizing for action. The new peasant talks like this:

> *Francisco:* We want to change the situation, we don't want to live in complete misery anymore. We all have a right to Honduran lands. That is the mission we have to change our lives.

> *Julio:* Some were afraid, others said we were crazy, that we were communists, that we'd go to jail, that we'd end up in the cemetery. But we are the people, we are the owners of this earth.

> *Father Roberto:* A peasant described it like this: "The peasant is like the temple that has been desecrated, and our farm organizations are driving the thieves from the temple to restore the dignity of the small farmer."

Few peasants talked like this 20 years ago. There are at least three things which have brought the change about. The first is the gradual land squeeze as the result of population increase and subdivision of lands; the second is the sudden land squeeze as a result of abrupt changes in agricultural practices; and the third is the emergence in the 1960s of organizations devoted to crystallizing the needs of the peasants and precipitating action.

A population growing at a rate of 3 percent per year doubles every 24 years. That is what has been happening in rural Honduras, and in the southern region, which is the nation's most densely populated, the peasant can actually perceive the change. The following comments were volunteered by Honduran peasant leaders in the course of general conversations on the land.

> *Andrés:* The land has not increased but the people have. We don't fit anymore. It is getting desperate.

> *Juan:* Here the land is scarce and the families big. Look, we're full of children—every father has eight children! I've got eight, and no land.

> *Francisco:* The families go on growing, so big that in time we won't be able to live with one another.

> *Lucas:* There are places where the people have multiplied. They have increased so much that there's not enough to live on.

> *Modesto:* The people were fertile and were producing big families, and there wasn't enough land.

As a consequence of more intensive agriculture without fertilizer or conservation practices, the fertility of the land in southern

Some were afraid, others said we were crazy, that we were communists, that we'd go to jail, that we'd end up in the cemetery. But we are the people, we are the owners of this earth.

JULIO

Honduras has declined so rapidly that virtually every peasant we spoke to had noticed it. Here are a few of their comments:

> *Pedro:* Today we work harder and have smaller harvests. The lands are tired.
>
> *Andrés:* The land was richer and produced more before. It's because we burn it.
>
> *Benigno:* I have a manzana of land and have never fertilized it. It's useless now, except for the animals. The land was good. when I was young. Now it's ruined.
>
> *Bernardo:* The harvests were much better before. I remember my father's harvests of rice compared with what I get now.

New sources of credit have emerged in the past decade, but the main ones do not reach the small farmer. As one peasant put it: "To get a loan you have to put something down, a cow, something. But I've got nothing and the bank won't help me even though I know what to do. That system helps the ones who already have it. The bank doesn't help the poor." Thus, the capital necessary to maintain land productivity under increasingly intensive use has been lacking, even where the farmer has the requisite knowledge and will.

Sociologist Robert White told us that the change has occurred within one generation. "Poverty is definitely increasing," he said. "Maybe the figures show that per-capita income is increasing but we find that in rural communities here where there were 20 families farming the land 25 years ago, the sons had to divide this land for their small subsistence plots, and there might be 70, 80, or 90 families trying to live off the same amount of land as they had 20 to 30 years ago."

The peasant, of course, had little enough land to begin with. Indeed, when we asked an official of Honduras's Peasant Association about the problem of land division he answered angrily: "We've visited 3,200 rural communities and haven't seen *that* problem. That's a problem for the capitalist landlord. The peasant's problem is that he has *no* land!"

As if the population increase and land tenure situation were not bad enough, the land situation has been further aggravated by peasants losing rights to land they traditionally utilized, land taken over in the past 20 years by the expansion of plantation crops such as cotton, sugar, and coffee, or by enclosure movements on the part of large cattle producers. In some cases, especially the cattlemen, they have simply moved into national or community lands and fenced out the small farmers; in others they have bought, rented or put under cultivation land previously available to peasants through custom. In El Salvador, a coffee grower tells how times have changed in one generation:

> Thirty years ago our coastal region was almost a forest, and the landlords only used them for lumber, leaving the people to pick the fruit and gather their firewood. Then came the cotton

Two out of three farms are less than two acres.

fever and the landlords converted those woods for cotton exploitation. Now the people can't find a stick of firewood or a fruit that is free to pick. Also the small farmer could always get permission to build his rancho on such lands, but now many landowners have expelled people who had been living for 30 or 50 years on land now planted with cotton.

In the north of Honduras we visited a farmer in an area where sugar cane was now occupying land previously rented at low rates to subsistence farmers. He told us rather bitterly: "Before we could grow corn, but now they rent to sugar growers. All this land used to be cultivated, but the señor has put in cattle and now there's no place to grow anything."

In the south of Honduras the situation is much more critical. "The landlords," a Honduran researcher told us, have been enclosing lands, pushing the small farmer up the hills, while the landowner uses the rich bottomland appropriate for agriculture to pasture his cattle." When cotton prices rose in the fifties, Salvadorans and Nicaraguans short of land in their own countries moved into southern Honduras to rent land for cotton production. The situation was well summarized by Father Robert White, a Cornell-trained sociologist:

> About fifteen years ago cotton and cattle production was accelerated in southern Honduras. The large land owners began to take over large sections of national land, land owned by the government, and evicted many of the small farmers. Not only were they evicted, but they found they couldn't rent land. The large land owners controlled the Supreme Court and the national Congress. It was sheer desperation. The small farmers were going hungry and once they organized they risked not being hired by the cotton producers!

The last two sentences show how futile is the attempt on the part of the small farmer to resist unless he is backed by strong organizations. His situation is comparable to an urban worker who goes on strike without a union to back him. With subsistence food at stake, the risks are indeed high, as shown by the following instance, in which a farm cooperative member relates incidents which had occurred only 15 days previously in the community of El Corpus:

> The engineer told us the land was national land, that belonged to the *municipio*. So we cleared the land and raised corn on it, and then when we harvested it the head of the hacienda sent a commission and put us in jail. They waited and took the harvest and left us with nothing. Imagine, with the price of corn where it is now!

In this instance the story may have a relatively happy ending—a lawyer from the Agrarian Reform Institute got the farmers released on bail and a surveyor is reverifying the ownership of the lands—but only because a powerful governmental organization is willing and able to assist. It is the emergence of these private and public groups in the past decade which give the peasant movement a fighting chance.

> In our village a meeting was unknown before. We went to Mass but we didn't work together. Now they know what it is to love one another. Now the people like organization.

9
Banana:
The Golden Fruit

The arrival of the banana companies constituted a second colonization for Honduras. . . . Sixty percent of the nation's best lands are in the hands of two foreign companies.

MARCO VIRGILIO CARÍAS,

One out of every four of the world's bananas is grown in Central America, and most Central American bananas are grown in Honduras. In earlier decades bananas accounted for close to 90 percent of the nation's exports and still account for over half. Moreover, by every standard of *per capita* welfare, the banana plantations of Honduras's north coast approach perfection. A combination of highly efficient agricultural technology, steady markets, and a recently developed progressive social consciousness yield both high wages and unusual social benefits for the worker. The Standard Fruit Company, for example, can boast a $1.5 million-profit per year, while it pays its 4,000 workers several times the average wage. According to the company's division manager, "Average earnings per family unit are approaching $2,000 per year, which for anyone familiar with Latin America is a fairly impressive statistic. The average for a single worker is $1,500, and if you add the housing, hospital, and other fringe benefits the real earnings are over $2,000. The average Honduran worker gets only $400. In fact, if you eliminate just the banana industry, the national average drops to $200!"

The fringe benefits are indeed substantial. Dr. Zepeda, head of medical services, told us that "more than 18,000 people in our work area are under control for infectious diseases." There are several hospitals and 14 dispensaries servicing the workers' medical needs. Social workers organize "housewives clubs" for nutrition, hygiene, and home economics education. Ninety-six teachers are employed in 21 schools with 3,600 children; and 40 teachers give adult education and literacy training in 22 "capacitation centers," designed to eliminate "the illiteracy or near-illiteracy of 3,000 workers." While most of the workers now live in less than ideal housing, the company hopes eventually to have all the workers own their own houses and has taken first steps in this direction.

To complete the worker's utopia, there are strong democratic and effective labor unions. Indeed, banana workers account for close to three-quarters of all union memberships in Honduras, and the AFL/CIO-trained staffs keep the pressure on the companies for wage and social benefits, while devising other types of economic and social benefits for the rank and file.

A crop which not only earns many export dollars but which provides such relative well-being for the workers would seem to be the basis for an agricultural paradise, but for two defects: the paradise is small, and it is shrinking. Despite the fact that bananas account for almost 30 percent of the nation's agricultural production, the industry employs no more than 1 percent of the nation's manpower. Moreover, in a period when the labor supply has been increasing at a rate of over 3 percent per year, the demand for labor has been declining.

The labor dilemma of a high-efficiency agro-industry operating in a highly competitive market is well analyzed by Standard's division manager in Honduras, Robert Fisher:

> Agricultural operations throughout the world have historically been labor intensive. Because of the nature of the banana business, it is still fairly labor intensive. But it's changing. Before, we were able to solve our problems either through hiring more people or through inefficiencies. Now, we have to have well-trained, permanent workers, not just somebody from the mountains or off the street.

The Harvard Business School graduate went on to explain how increased productivity essentially means fewer workers:

> The price received for bananas is about the same in retail stores as it was in 1948, while the cost of distribution in the States has risen sharply. Faced with this you either have to increase the productivity of your farms (your net product), which decreases your unit cost, or you increase productivity per worker.
>
> Only ten years ago all the fruit harvested was brought in by mules. Now it's all brought in by tractor. Five years ago we had about 450 people in maintenance of our railroads, and doing a very poor job. Now we have 150 and are completely mechanized.

Fisher explained that there were substantial reductions in labor force between 1960 and 1965; in the latter half of the decade "there have been few overall reductions in people, but we are getting more from the existing workforce."

The unions are understandably nervous about the future. They remember when the strikes and natural disasters of the fifties resulted in drastic reductions in the labor force. At the labor union serving United Fruit workers, we were told that within a few years prior to 1960 the labor force of 36,000 was reduced to 15,000 and subsequently reduced even more. At Standard Fruit, an official put the blame on the union:

> The strike and the unions had to come and it's probably for the best. Of course it brought in a certain amount of mechanization like everywhere else. We had about 12,000–13,000 laborers then and we're down to 5,000 or so now. You had to, what with paid vacations, hospitalization, schooling, and housing. . . . Take how they used to control plant disease. It took quite a labor force, you had to spray every two weeks. But when the labor laws came along why you couldn't afford to have these 48 men dragging the hose down through the farms, so that put the airplane in business with the spray. [Elsewhere we were told that aerial crop dusting cost 2,800 jobs.]

The unions also see signs of new technology in packing and transport, which could cost many jobs. While both labor and management see a bright future for the average banana workers, nobody expects an increase in the number of workers who will enjoy their standard of living. It is a tiny, lush, and somewhat artificial island in a sea of impoverished workers, an island slowly eroding in size as the human tide around it steadily increases.

The banana used to be hauled by mule and there were a lot of muleteers. Then the wagon was introduced and fewer muleteers were needed. Then the tractor, and now a new cable device which will eliminate a lot of drivers.

The strike brought in a certain amount of mechanization as it did everywhere else. We had about 12,-000 to 13,000 laborers then and we're down to 5,000 or so now.

OFFICIAL, STANDARD FRUIT

No one in Latin America believes that the mere distribution of land to the peasants will go far in solving the land problem. It is customary to add that improved technology and organization are needed along with land. The cooperative (consumer, production, or marketing) is an organization of farmers which expedites the adoption of technical innovations, pools resources, and generates the political power and psychic rewards characteristic of organized groups. Thus when Rigoberto Sandoval, head of Honduras's National Agrarian Institute (INA) told us that "land reform must be a movement from the bottom to the top," he was talking about the need to organize the peasants at the bottom. When he took credit for benefiting "17,000 families in the past two years," he was careful to point out that only about 2,300 of these families yet had the benefit of fully organized cooperatives, and it was clear that in his mind the co-op was the real objective.

What does such organization mean to the peasant? As the illustrations from three co-op members show, it means everything from eliminating the middleman to beginning to feel like a human being.

> I had land I was working, but when I sold the harvest the "coyotes" paid me $10 and sold it for $100. I thought the cooperative would solve this problem of marketing.
>
> They used to say the cooperative was communism; now we realize the rich go around saying that so the poor won't unite and defend themselves.*
>
> We started to work, we started to feel, we started to understand that it was necessary to organize and change our way of life . . . that we had a right to eat better, earn more, live better. If there's no sustenance there's no life and that's what we Hondurans were fighting for. Every human being has a right to subsist, doesn't he?

Despite the handful of organized members, Sandoval was optimistic about the cooperatives. He pointed out that "the average peasant family earns $230 per year, but in some of our cooperatives income jumped to $1,185 within 15 months. This has affected only about 2,500 families now, but we're moving fast." He was especially sanguine about the Guanchias cooperatives where INA is putting its most concerted efforts and where about 900 families have joined. The cooperatives trace their origins to the 1954 banana workers strike, after which plant diseases and floods, plus increasing pressure from an Alliance for Progress–oriented government, caused the banana companies to abandon land which could be taken over by small producers or by cooperatives, who in turn sell their produce to the companies.

In other instances the government tried to reclaim natural lands which had been gradually taken over by large cattle producers. In the mid-sixties Dr. Ricardo Pozas observed that "the cattlemen have invaded the lands of the cooperatives, fencing them with barbed wire. The cooperative members are continually

10
The
Cooperative

122

menaced by the armed forces, who permit the cattlemen to bear arms but prohibit the peasants from doing so. The local authorities also protect the cattlemen while attacking the cooperatives."* Subsequently the *campesinos* dramatically removed the fencing, and in mid-1968 the first crops were planted by the cooperative members. The economic vicissitudes of a 112-member cooperative are well summarized by its president:

> We had no land, and after petitioning INA we got 340 manzanas. We started to cultivate corn but the prices were very unstable and we had to sell at a very low price. We were failing, but we increased cultivation to 700 manzanas. Again we failed. There was great desperation in that period. Then Sandoval took over and negotiated with Standard Fruit for bananas. Now we are hopeful . . .

But the struggle is by no means over, economically or politically. The division manager of Standard Fruit gave the following opinion on the viability of the cooperatives:

> We signed contracts with them and provide them a considerable amount of technical support. We really only began a couple of years ago and we're just getting into production now. It's a little early to say, but we're optimistic. You still need tremendous technical assistance and they will require the support of our research facilities, shops, and that sort of thing. . . . The large cooperatives are not paying anywhere near what our workers earn—probably a third. How they will be able to operate when they do start paying higher wages, how efficiently will depend on how we coordinate our supervision. . . . Trying to run a banana farm with a hundred bosses instead of one is not an easy task but we think it can be done.

Thus, with all the advantages of unusually fertile soil, a ready and accessible market, an expensive infrastructure of railroads, drainage, irrigation, etc., provided by the companies, technical assistance from a modern multimillion-dollar organization on the one hand and the experts of the National Agrarian Institute on the other, the economic viability of the handful of pioneering cooperatives is still in question. But this may be one of the less immediate of the cooperatives' worries; before they prosper they must win still other kinds of battles. An emotion-choked banana cutter described the risks involved:

> On the 17th day of April, 1966, our cooperative was organized. On the 5th of May, engineer Piñeda was murdered. Last week another worker was murdered for our cause.
> A bunch of soldiers took me out of my house and threatened to kill me. The month before last our five cooperatives were accused and we had to pay plenty to lawyers and others. We are threatened and abused, all because we want to change our way of life, from a backward system we can't take anymore.

Sandoval had told us "there is no land reform without blood," and his words were well chosen. In September of 1970 a landowner was in jail on suspicion of murdering Sandoval's right-hand man.

11
The Colonization

Throughout Latin America the most frequently heard solution to the population problem is to move people from densely settled areas to the sparsely settled ones. Since there are far more of the latter than the former, most Latins cannot develop much concern about present or future population size. Few governments have actually tried to move people, and with good reason. It is difficult and expensive—and it runs against a migratory tide in the other direction. We were surprised, then, to hear about a bold experiment of this kind in Honduras, where the National Agrarian Institute (INA) had uprooted a group from a depressed and densely settled district and moved them to a newly purchased hacienda called San Bernardo. The initial motivation came from a group of peasants in the densely populated southern region of Honduras, where a combination of population growth, subdivision of land, and enclosure movements by cotton and cattle farmers created both land scarcity and land degeneration. The peasants in a number of communities had been agitating for land parcelization over the past few years, and one of them, Modesto Dominguez, was convinced that their only hope was in leaving the region for new lands. When we met Dominguez we asked him why. "We had land," he said, "but it was bad land that didn't produce, and the landlords took half the crop we harvested on their land. Then the middleman took his share. He bought the harvest, then the peasant had to buy it back at a high price. So we made a petition to INA and they moved us."

But this was no simple move. INA poured an incredible amount of resources into the venture. They expropriated the 3,500-hectare Hacienda San Bernardo from a Nicaraguan, cattle and all, and promised to pay $400,000 for it. They marshaled army trucks to move the peasants, secured family-sized tents for temporary housing, convinced CARITAS to donate 6,000 pounds of food, loaned the settlers $15,000 for equipment, invested $44,000 in improving the infrastructure, and provided a civil engineer, agronomists, cooperative extension technicians, and a cattle expert.

Thus far we seem to have a simple story with a happy ending: peasants are hungry, forceful grassroots leader makes demands, government provides money and technical assistance, peasants, no longer hungry, are happy and productive. But the story is not so simple nor the ending so happy. To understand why INA jumped hard and fast when petitioned, we must first understand that the general region which Modesto Dominguez represents has been seething with peasant unrest over the past five years. As just one example, we cite Robert White's recent history of the farmers who have been living on land bordering the Hacienda San

Bernardo:

For years the small farmers of Azacualpas had been moving into the area bordering the Hacienda San Bernardo to make their milpas and they gradually were establishing permanent homes there. They had always considered the land to be national and open for occupation. In the early 1950s, at the beginning of the cotton and cattle boom, the owner of the hacienda fenced in the whole area, had the settlers there removed by force, and jailed any who resisted the removal.

The small subsistence farmers planted their milpas in land outside the property of the Hacienda San Bernardo, but the owner ordered all the fences in the area taken down and took possession of the land surrounding the hacienda. In view of this action, several of the small farmers of the area presented a writ of injunction before the Supreme Court. The court declared against them and in favor of the landowner. The whole movement was set in motion by the farmers of the neighborhood without any formal organization.

In 1954, by order of the Ministry of Government, some fifty families were evicted from their plots. It was a case of public office acting in collusion with the powerful against the small farmer. The land was largely utilized in cotton production rather than in basic grains. The owner did not personally manage the hacienda but rented out more than 700 manzanas of land at the price of $40 per manzana. Much of the land was used extensively in the pasture of cattle. (Later, when the land was expropriated, it was discovered that most of it was national land.)

In the mid-1950s the whole neighborhood was fenced in with barbed wire and the farmers had to crawl through fences to get to water or to the school. They were forbidden to collect kindling in the area and various men were accused of stealing wood and were jailed by order of the owner. The plantings of bananas and the fruit trees that some of the families had put in were destroyed.

The movements of the fifties were spontaneous and unorganized; in the sixties organized protest began. The newly established National Association of Honduran Peasants (ANACH) sent an organizer to the south, where the Cattle Growers Association (AGASH) promptly had him thrown in jail. Organized pressure brought his release, and a local affiliate of the Peasant Organization was triumphantly formed in 1967. Over the next two years the peasants directed petitions at INA calling for rectification of the situation at San Bernardo. Frustrated by INA's failure to act, they invaded the San Bernardo property in April, 1969, claiming that these were national lands, and setting a precedent: this was the first land invasion in southern Honduras. Disarmed of their machetes and ordered to leave by the national army, they held fast; they demanded and got an interview with INA director Sandoval, who promised action in August. The war with El Salvador intervened, but hopes were raised when in September an engineer was seen surveying the hacienda lands reputed to be national lands. It was discovered that there were indeed 6,000 acres of national land in addition to 3,500 owned by the Nicaraguan. INA now had much more than it needed—a crisis, a foreign landowner, a just case of misuse of national lands. In a sweeping move it both recovered the national lands and expropriated the private ones. With this much land and the makings of an infrastructure (the hacienda house, roads, etc.), it could open up San Bernardo as a model for production cooperatives, and could actually *transport* populations from neighboring areas as a superdramatic evidence of land resettlements. It seized on Modesto Dominguez's request for relocation of his group, and poured in money and manpower for the fifty-odd families Dominguez led as to a promised land.

Of the various cooperatives established on the San Bernardo property, only one had been composed of new settlers. While the others were painfully making a modicum of progress, Modesto's community, bravely named Nueva Concepción, seemed in trouble. When we visited the settlers in the summer of 1970, a few months after their arrival, disillusion was setting in. Still living in tents, far from the nearest village, the children racked with a new wave of respiratory and intestinal illnesses, they listened listlessly as an extension specialist lectured them on the historic underpinnings of the cooperative movement in Europe and complained that Modesto was ruling them as if they were children. A month later the German engineer who was to help them build their houses and roads quit, a number of the settlers had returned to their original homes, and Modesto was in jail. Six months later the dynamic leader of INA was replaced.

> **Few governments have tried to move people. It is difficult, expensive, and running against a migratory tide that is moving in the other direction.**

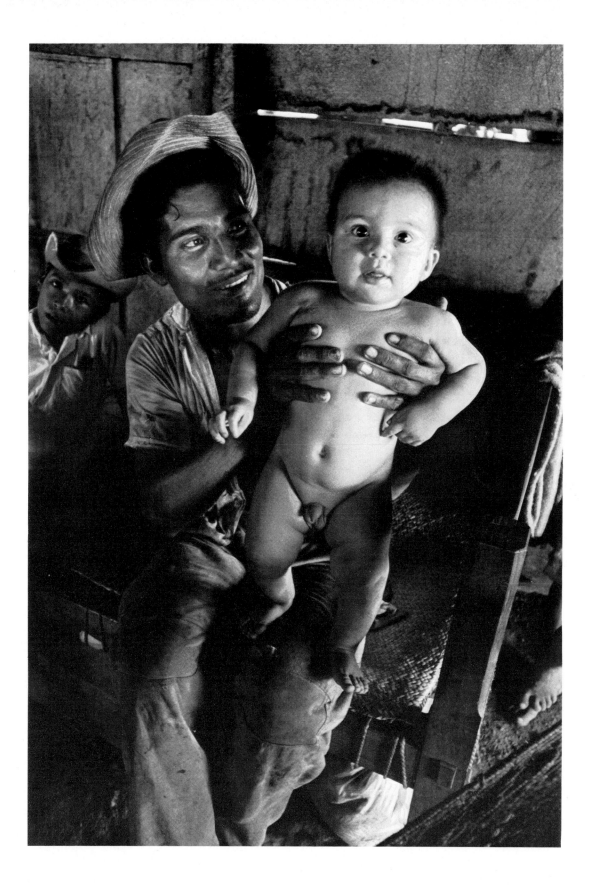

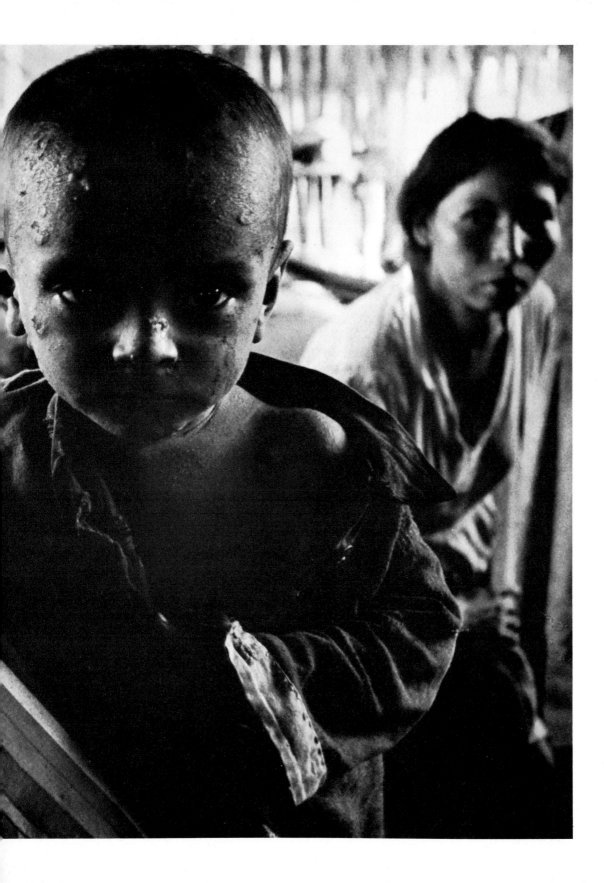

Ideologies and Programs

When did it start?

In that partly decaying, partly ossifying spiritual Gargantua known as the Roman Catholic Church, when did the change begin? A Honduran government official had a simple answer: "They were desperate. They haven't done anything for so many years that now they want to move fast." They have a long way to go. Nineteenth-century anticlericalism was successful in pushing the Church out of direct and active participation in public affairs, while the growth of new urban classes and more aggressive Protestantism increasingly challenged the Church's spiritual monopoly. Earlier in this century, the "social apostolate" philosophy of clerical engagement with human problems was emphasized by a minority of the clergy, but most remained quite removed from the larger social and economic problems facing Latin Americans. But in the last few decades there have been major stirrings for reform in the Church which culminated in the early 1960s with the liturgical and theological reforms of Vatican II. In 1967 Pope Paul VI released the encyclical *Populorium progressio* condemning certain aspects of capitalist societies, especially in relation to poor countries. But for Latin America the turning point was in August, 1968, when the Latin American Conference of Bishops meeting at Medellín, Colombia, put its stamp of approval on the notion of the Church as an instrument of social change. If few joined with the Colombian priest Camilo Torres in proclaiming that "the duty of the Christian is to make the revolution," the term "theology of development" began to be heard more often as well as increasing references to the "marginal" existence of most of Latin America's people. "For the Catholic," a lay religious leader in Honduras told us, "Christian social involvement and the solution of social and economic problems are not options but commitments. We cannot conceive a Church any more that is only interested in spiritual things." Bishop Marcelo Gerin seemed to agree. "Here in Honduras," he said, "I feel that a new Christianity is taking shape—justice and love in action."

"Man made society and man has to change it," said another priest in the South of Honduras. "We want a change in the way a person sees himself, from being passive to becoming an active agent in his own betterment, so that he can take from Honduras what he should take, and give Honduras what he should give."

This insistence on the *religious* duty of the Christian to become an active agent in social change is what is so startling to hear from a Church long cast as an agent of social stability, rendering to God only "the things that were God's." One young priest explained the older traditions of the Church as an adaptation to the hopelessness of poverty. "There's never been an age in which the Church hasn't felt a special mission to the poor," he explained. "They developed a theology of tolerance, of putting up with it,

12
New Men
of the Cloth

Those in the forefront of the struggle for radical, even revolutionary, reform in Latin America today are more likely to be found wearing Roman collars than carrying red banners.

SENATOR FRANK CHURCH

perhaps because they didn't know how to conquer the poverty of the people." Whatever the roots, there is little doubt about the change. "The Church here in Latin America has taught these people resignation," Father Santana told us, "that it's good to be poor and it's good to be miserable in this world because we're going to have our recompense in the other world. . . . Now we tell these people the only way to get to heaven is to work here on earth to help our brothers."

But if Medellín was long on words, it was short on action programs. "With 50 percent of our people illiterate," explained Mexican Bishop Ruiz Garcia, "confronted by a population explosion, with a clergy that does not renew itself (let alone increase in number), with an antiquated financial organization and a population scattered over mountains, plains, and jungles, it was not easy to implement our conference declarations."

The south of Honduras is a good place to see Medellín in action. Largely under the leadership of Canadian missionary priests, a movement called Acción Cultural Popular Hondureña (ACPH) is a loosely organized collection of activities blending Christian principles with social action. Its leadership is turned out at an impressive training center called "La Colmena" (The Hive), its voice is a radio station which both teaches literacy and inculcates a social consciousness, its right arm is a religious movement known as "Celebration of the Word," and its left arm a small army of grass roots community organizers.

"Celebración de la Palabra" is an evangelical type of religious revival; laymen conduct the Sunday worship, in which the congregation participates actively and in which social themes are encouraged for discussion or sermonizing. In each of several hundred communities, three "delegates" (lay ministers) have been selected and trained. They are often grass roots leaders, and the new religious authority vested in them has encouraged them to increase their involvement with community affairs. We asked one delegate what "Celebracion de la Palabra" has meant for him, and his reply showed the new mixture of religious and worldly concerns: "In our village a meeting was unknown before. We went to Mass but we didn't understand the Mass. The people were individuals, they didn't work together. Now they know what it is to love one another. Now the people like organization."

The radio schools, initiated in the early 1960s, are even more directly linked to social action. The special feature of the radio schools is their extension into the community by means of "monitors." Like the delegates (and they are often the same person), monitors are selected from the ranks of the poor farmers; after being trained, they meet monthly for refresher work. They are now at work in 600 communities. They are expected to organize listening groups, such as literacy groups, youth groups, and house-

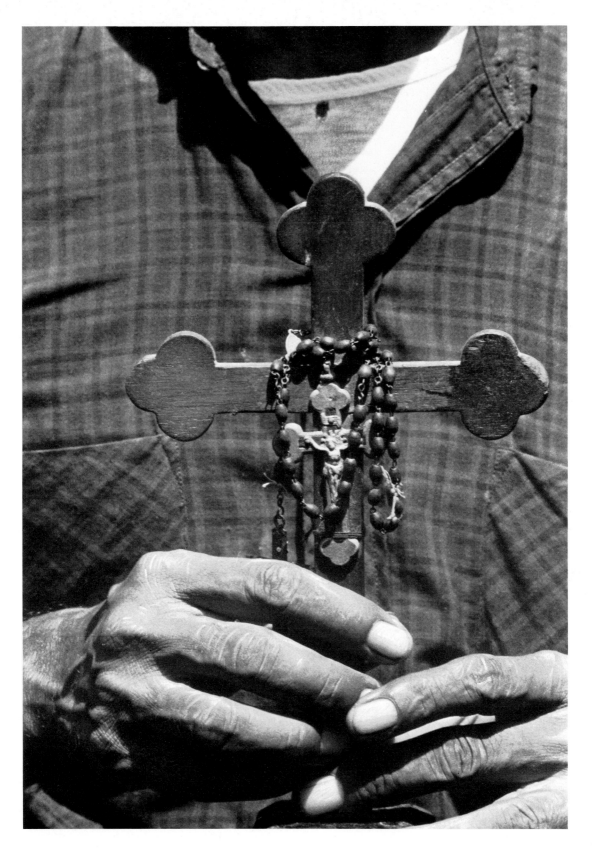

wives groups, corresponding to the programs transmitted by Radio Paz. Monitors are subsequently converted to *promotores* (community organizers) by a three-week training course.

Even the literacy classes are laced with concepts to create "awareness" on the part of the listener. "We're not just teaching literacy," says ACPH leader Fernando Montes, "although we've taught 50,000 people to read and write. What we want most is social, economic, and political change in the life of the *campesinos*. So instead of teaching them the word *'puerta'* we teach them *'pobreza'* (poverty), and instead of teaching *'tomate'* we teach them *'tecnica,'* and how technical skills are lacking in peasant cultivation."

By organized community action, 175 kilometers of roads have been constructed and 200 schools built. In one instance seven communities pulled together, marshaled financial assistance from AID, elicited community labor, and built a much-needed road connecting the villages. Father Pablo Gurellet, director of the training center at "La Colmena," gave us his view of what such activity does psychologically for the poor. "They no longer think that their failure is due to their individual shortcomings," he said. "They move from 'I'm no good for anything' to 'We're all in the same boat.' Through the process of group meetings they come to feel, 'Now I understand that our problems, my problems, and those of the community, are problems of all small farmers in Honduras.'"

"Our biggest problem is to create a people, to create an awareness," said one of the peasants who had become an instructor. "We want them convinced that change is not something that will come from 'out there' but from below, from within." "Lack of unity is the chief problem of these communities" said Father Santana. "The day we find unity we'll find a way to overcome ignorance and hunger."

Building up self-esteem, creating an awareness of the social nature of their problems, dispelling pluralistic ignorance, and instilling brotherhood and unity are the objectives. How it works is told simply by a peasant leader:

> A Canadian priest came here and made me a radio monitor. I felt ashamed, me with only one year of school, but he gave me courage. "You can learn and teach," he said, and I've been doing that for years, and we teach everyone, even the old ones.

The speaker has done more than his words suggest. He is Modesto Dominguez, described in Chapter 14 as one of the more successful peasant leaders.

The organizers move on to establish credit and savings cooperatives and an occasional production cooperative; eventually they cooperate with such direct action agencies as the peasant leagues. In one way or another they can then pressure the government for action on land reform, and the government agency responsible for it (INA) finds them to be "a disciplined people, an evangelized people," according to one of the leaders, "a people who will help INA to move."

It should not be thought, however, that because priests are behind the movement it escapes the attacks of the establishment. Robert White documents the way in which there is currently an open conflict between the radio school cooperative and the controlling political party in one community.*

"Use of school buildings for the radio school meetings or other clubs has been prohibited," he writes, and "rural school teachers who frequently get their jobs through political connections and payoffs have given almost no direct help to the radio school system. The supervisor of education has openly declared himself to be against the radio school movement . . . arguing that the priests have prostituted the church building by giving premar-

riage courses there. . . . The mayor will have nothing to do with the priests. 'They have changed our religion and are a bunch of rascals,' he says. 'They are promoting peasant leagues and furthermore are turning the people against me.' "

Moreover, the pace of change is slow where so many things need to be changed at once. A good example is literacy. "The effectiveness in raising literacy has not really met our expectations," says White. "Once the *campesino* knows how to read and write, he has no newspaper, no magazines, no books coming into the home."

As to the broad panoply of social and economic life, this is the way it was, as described by Sister Marta Peletier, at the beginning of the Church's work:

> This mass of 38,000 persons lived isolated, abandoned, almost like the animals which slept in their houses; poor diets, disease, naked children; no roads, illiteracy, the woman a slave to the vices of the man who leaves her with two or three children to go on to other women.

Now there is hope and the beginnings of social action. But when we asked Father Normand if he had noticed any significant changes in the level of living since his work there he answered wistfully, "Not really. But then, I have only been here for five years."

In El Salvador, land reform is even less advanced than in Honduras; and when a congress of land reform was held in the legislative assembly during January of 1970, it attracted a good deal of attention. Part of the reason was a fiery young priest named José Alas who insisted that agrarian reform move past the talking stage, and who demanded that unionization of the peasants be permitted. We visited Father Alas in his Spartan room in Suchitoto, and he told us what happened next: "On January 8 a group of four men kidnapped me and left me drugged and naked on a mountain. I spent nine days unconscious in a hospital after being found. . . . In 1932, 25,000 peasants were killed here in the name of the struggle against communism. As you can see, in El Salvador action is quite violent, both against the peasant and against those who try to awaken him."

The archbishop reacted strongly to the kidnapping, excommunicated its "intellectual and material authors," and created a great deal of publicity for Father Alas, who is now trying to mobilize the peasants in his 37,000-soul parish. He draws as frequently on the Medellin Bishops' Proclamation as on the Bible, and is fond of citing the bishops' promise "to denounce energetically the abuses and injustices stemming from the excessive inequalities between rich and poor, the powerful and the weak." Accordingly, in his sermons, Father Alas continually reminds the peasants of the discrepancy between what they are and what they should be, between what they have and what they should have. "Man is not free in parts," he has said. "We cannot speak of liberty if his body is suffering. Hunger, ill-health, illiteracy, and lack of housing conspire against our liberty. How can our nation celebrate Independence Day while children are dying of hunger and men cannot read and write?"

"When we say 'Our Father' we mean the Father of *all* of us," he said in another sermon; "and when we say 'Give us this day our daily bread,' that bread is for *everyone*."

In case religious analogies seem too vague, Father Alas frequently utilizes simple but valid statistical concepts. "In this country," he explained to a group of parishioners, "when we produce a hundred pesos, eight people take 92 of those pesos and 92 people get the eight. And the same with land. . . . But God has ordered that Man dominate the earth. And that doesn't mean individuals, it means *Man*."

This leads him to his major theme, the agrarian reform. In 1970 an important law was passed which, if expedited, could result in significant changes in Salvadoran land tenure. Father Alas is making sure his parishioners understand its implications.

What is *munifundio?* It's what you have and are fighting for, a small plot in the hands of a family. But the *munifundio* is no good, and agrarian reform is against it because it produces a

13
The Church
Militant

> . . . It is not that we are asking for land. What we want is that there be a place to work. . . . That is why many steal, because there is no land for them. Through land reform we can gain our freedom; we are not asking for lands but for freedom to be able to live.
>
> PADRE ALAS

To love Christianity dreaming of heaven is to forget this earth which is also of God.

PADRE ALAS

subsistence economy. That means a man, his wife and four or five kids have only enough land to live off of, but not enough to sell any produce. A country full of *munifundios* would be a poor country. Agrarian reform doesn't want that. Neither do they want *latifundios*—the big land holding—in the hands of a few people. But *you* could have a *latifundio*—run it as a co-operative. Together you could have a tractor, cultivate two or three hundred manzanas. That is land reform!

During the period that we visited Father Alas a significant issue on land reform was brewing, and the priest was using it as a concrete means of mobilizing the peasants into some form of group action. A private company called Rural Land Parcels, backed by some of the wealthiest landlords, has recently been formed in order to purchase large tracts of underutilized land, divide it into medium-sized plots, and provide capital and technical assistance to make these plots highly productive. A million dollars have already been subscribed for this purpose, and there is little doubt that more rational, productive and diversified agriculture will result from the plan. There is one small defect, however. Since it is essentially a profit-making enterprise, it must ignore the penniless peasant in favor of the medium-sized farmer who can raise the necessary capital or credit. In some circumstances this could hurt the small farmer who has traditionally been permitted to live on the underexploited lands of the large hacendado, but who would certainly have to move when such land was taken over by a medium-sized farmer seeking to rationalize his holding.

In a decision which can be ascribed only to God or the devil, the company's first purchase was 1,600 manzanas of land owned by the Hacienda Asunción, deep in the territory of Father Alas, who quickly perceived that the 86 peasant families living on the property were in danger of being expelled. As a consequence he has had a number of meetings, some of them held defiantly on the lands of Hacienda Asunción in which the company has been denounced for policies which will force the people off the land. By November of 1970 their activities had had the unprecedented effect of attracting the visit of a commission of the National Assembly, who met with the peasant leaders and promised to "weigh the evidence." The company was also considering special prices for the *colonos*, but these prices will almost certainly be beyond the reach of most of them.

With an emotional but realistic issue now available, Father Alas is operating at top form, and illustrates the new face of the Church Militant. Instead of exhorting the faithful to patience and humility, in sermons and in mimeographed broadsides he exhorts them to be brave, strong, and free. "There is a pyramid of oppression," he writes in his newsletter, "at whose base the hungry, sick, and naked peasant is intimidated by such tendentious phrases as 'You'll be accused of communism! We'll call the

militia! Seek Eternal Salvation! Give thanks to God if your child
dies of hunger—he will go to heaven!' There are too many
Christians who go to Communion but avoid community organization; who are afraid to join the peasant leagues or the workers
movement. To live Christianity dreaming of heaven is to forget
this earth, which is also of God."

"Be men," he exhorted them in a sermon we listened to. "Be
sure and united men! Fear nothing. It is better to lose your skin
fighting than lose with your head bowed. Because sooner or later
we will die anyway. Better to lose fighting and leave a better
world for your children."

Father Alas practices what he preaches. We noted the rifle in
the corner of his little room, the shells on the bookcase, the re-
volver under his pillow.

14
Population
and
Birth Control

If population growth in Central America were to cease tomorrow, none of the nations' problems of poverty would go away—but they would be somewhat easier to solve if the population were not doubling every twenty years. By now, most Americans accept this point of view as "logical and obvious," forgetting how controversial it was only a decade ago. In Honduras and El Salvador it is not only still highly controversial, but is now inextricably entwined with deeper political issues.

HONDURAS

Dr. Axel Mundigo of Cornell University recently surveyed the opinions of 300 Honduran decision makers—divided fairly evenly among government officials, lawyers, and leaders in industry and commerce. Eighty percent of them had had a university education, and close to two-thirds spoke a language other than Spanish, usually English. Each was asked what were the three most important problems facing Honduras; of the roughly 900 citations, only six referred to population growth. When asked if Honduras had a population problem, two-thirds said it did not; and when asked whether Honduras' present population size was adequate, almost three-quarters said it was not.* Further queried on the desirability of a national family-planning program to reduce the growth rate, half flatly opposed it, and only a third agreed without reservation. Those who were opposed to such a program were asked if they would favor it if it were aimed at reducing the high rate of abortion. The ratio of negative to positive responses was almost two to one. Examples are taken from four interviews:

A former Cabinet member and current deputy in the legislature: The development of a nation is in direct proportion to the volume of its population—the more consumers, the more business. Hondurans are only half populating this country, and it is logical that more Hondurans are needed to develop it, and to defend its sovereignty and territorial integrity. The powerful nations want to keep the hungry people of the world from being born, or want them to die as soon as possible. This justifies their world campaign for family planning and their stimulation of local wars. To kill the unborn is equivalent to destroying the living. Man is born with his own capacity to produce his food. It is up to the state to give him the means to realize this capacity. Honduras needs more soldiers for its defense against a populous enemy who seeks our depopulation by means of the bullet or the pill.

A Lawyer: Honduras has no population problem, since its population is insignificant in relation to our territory, and since it has the necessary resources, if exploited by private industry, assisted by the state. . . . Family planning would weaken our economy. It's the peasant and workers' families who sustain agriculture and industry. Thus, family planning would diminish our principal factor in production—the worker and the small farmer—and make us vulnerable to any overpopulated nation.

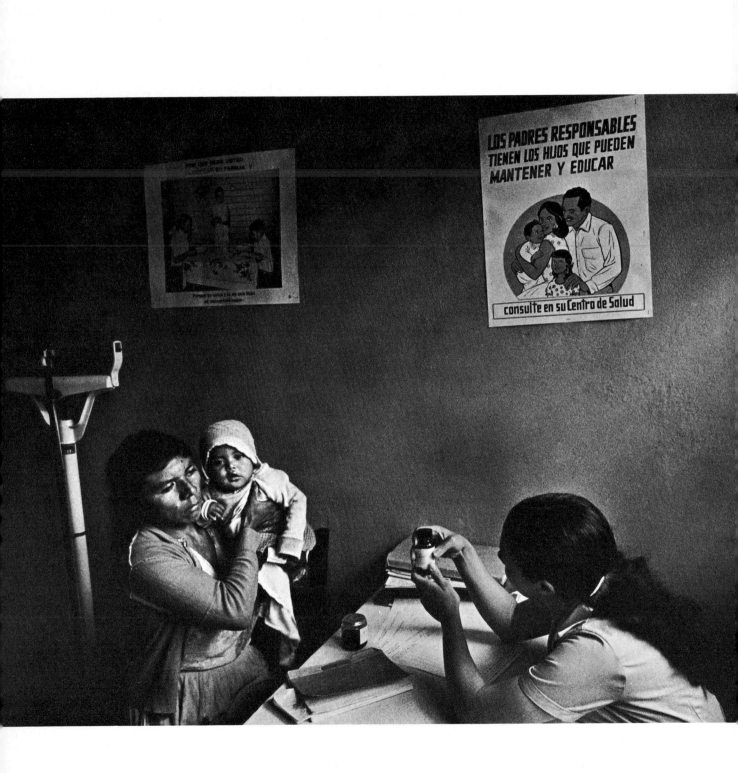

A Ministry of Health official: I have five reasons for being opposed to family planning: (1) It brings underpopulation, which is already a serious problem in our country; (2) it leads to family disintegration, converting the woman into an object of sexual satisfaction; (3) the woman could develop cancer and there are no good studies on effects of the IUD— also unknown is the effect on the chromosomes; (4) the pill has produced an increase in prostitution in Honduras; and (5) the pill is an example of foreign techniques applied to an environment culturally unprepared to receive them.

A union official: I disagree with the men of science who would prevent a life from being, when it is easier to increase the number of schools and jobs. . . . God gave man the mission to increase and multiply. . . . The woman who uses birth control is destroying and corrupting herself. . . . Birth control impoverishes nations with respect to human rights and human resources. If the population declines and manpower becomes scarce, then industry will have to mechanize.

What of the younger generation? "The University is completely closed to us," a leader in family planning told us. "From the president to the janitor they all have the same view." A survey of university student attitudes by Landstreet and Mundigo shows that while this generalization was overdrawn, opposition to family planning on demographic grounds was considerable. Four hundred students at the National University filled out questionnaires in 1970, and were classified according to their political ideology (see Table D).

Only a minority of students believe that population growth hurts economic development, or favor a national program of family planning.* As one moves left in the political spectrum, the attitude toward population as a problem becomes increasingly negative. While a small minority, the radical left is the best organized and most effective political voice in most Central American universities, and in Honduras had been responsible for circulating many leaflets with messages such as these:

Hondurans: The Yankee imperialists want fewer Hondurans in favor of the Salvadorans. We must make war against its programs of "Family Planning and Birth Control." Honduras needs more Hondurans.

Honduran Women: Don't ruin your health participating in the Birth Control Program. It is a gringo trick to depopulate our beloved country, in favor of the Salvadorans.

A leftist student leader presented a relatively sophisticated rationale for the North American interest in family planning:

We have no overpopulation; the land area is sufficient for the present population or for a larger one. . . . If the peasants are given land and technical assistance they can support their children satisfactorily. The nation needs more young people to put to work. Revolutionary movements are led by young people, and the youth of the future are a threat to the monopolistic interests—they could be the motor for the revolution, and the United States does not want youth to become a majority in the nation.

| Table D |
| Attitudes of National University Students toward Population Problems, According to Political Leanings, 1970 |

	Center	Right	Pro-revolution	Radical left
Percent who believe population growth increases poverty	42	53	49	30
Percent who believe population growth hurts economic development	47	40	37	33
Percent who favor a national family planning program	38	38	32	22
Number of interviews	(80)	(55)	(224)	(36)

We have been able to convince a lot of the young doctors to stay away from family planning. We've convinced them that to carry out such a program is to act against the nation. We have been able to force the medical school to suspend all birth control activity. The medical school will never allow a plan of North American penetration to be carried out in its name!

The student was not engaging in idle boasting. A professor gave us the following description of the university situation:

> The left believes that increasing poverty and misery is the only way to get the people to participate violently in a leftist revolution, and population growth is doing just that. We have had to cease totally any demographic work at the university. For example, the head of the department of preventive medicine has been under pressure not only to stop any teaching activities at the university, but outside the university as well. The topic is dead at the university. It cannot be discussed.

The net effect of strong opposition on the left and indifference to mild hostility to family planning on the right has been a national family-planning program which is very low-key. Although it was initiated at a government level as early as 1965 and now involves local funds as well as foreign, it is not reaching more than 2 percent of the women of childbearing age, and does its best to remain noiseless and invisible. As a doctor in the program put it:

> The campaign is failing because it hasn't made enough propaganda. I can assure you that 50 percent of the country people don't know it exists, and are unaware of any means to control their fertility. The malaria campaign was successful because they went house to house and made lots of propaganda. But this government is afraid of birth control.

Even the directors of the program deny that it has demographic objectives. They see it as a way of improving the health of mothers and children, and never mention its possible effect on the birth rate. Under these circumstances it would be surprising if it had any.

EL SALVADOR

Most Latin Americans regard density as the only problematic aspect of population growth, and in these terms there is a major difference between Honduras and El Salvador. It is a difference revealed not only by statistics—El Salvador has seven times as many people per square kilometer—it is a difference which is visible. As expressed by landowner Juan Wright:

> In Honduras you can travel enormous distances without seeing anyone. But I assure you that you couldn't answer a call of nature out in the open anywhere in El Salvador without being seen!

Wright went on to give his views on population and population control.

> . . . It's not that the father is irresponsible, but that he isn't earning enough to live; how can he be responsible without income?

I don't see how in 8,000 square miles over 5 million people can be fed—and that's what we'll have within ten years. We have no mines, no heavy industries. Maybe we can develop more assembly industries, maybe textiles, but to absorb 5 million people is our main problem. We need family planning so that increases in national income won't be diluted and the country won't move backward.

Coffee grower Romulo Leal also pointed out the unusual population density of El Salvador, and followed with an acute analysis of how the middle and upper classes view the population problem:

> The ignorant rich, landlords who live in the provinces, ignore the problem. They are like Louis XVI, who noted "nothing new" in his diary on July 14 (Bastille Day) because he didn't go hunting. They are totally blind to social problems. Their knowledge of what is happening here or in Cuba doesn't go beyond the newspaper headline.
>
> On the other hand, the landlord who lives in the capital is sophisticated. He knows if the demographic explosion continues we may have a tremendous revolution.
>
> In recent years middle-class people have fully realized the need for family planning, because life has been hard for them. It's taken a lot to get where they are, and they have come to the personal conviction that they can't afford the luxury of having so many children if those children are to achieve an economic status similar to their own. However, they have taken no initiative for a community program of family planning. It's the upper classes which have done this out of fear of the demographic explosion.

The upper class is by no means unanimous on this issue. A physician associated with the family-planning movement describes how the young people of the upper classes have tended to ignore the problem:

> I've been surprised by the absolute ignorance of these young people, especially the women, about the population problem and the availability of national resources. Most of them have been educated in the United States. They read *Time* and the *Miami Herald* instead of *Prensa Gráfica* or *Diario de Hoy*, and many have never in their lives been in our poor barrios. They view the problem in an idealistic way—you just have to increase production and everybody will eat!

Many conservative nationalists want a growing nation. A Monseigneur wrote recently:

> I am Salvadoran and I want my nation to progress harmoniously. I want Latin America to be big. The foreign monopolistic powers want to stop the growth of these peoples. The peoples who are nationalists, the most nationalistic, reject this birth control campaign as castration. [Diario de Hoy, 13 February 1970].

Perhaps the hemisphere's leading voice for a more populous Latin America is Napoleon Viera Altamirano, the rightist editor of El Salvador's *Diario de Hoy*. Over the past decade hundreds of

> **Having many children is a big problem at first but tomorrow if they are good and if they are lucky they can be a help. If they come out good it's a blessing from God. . . .**
> FARMER

his editorials have hurled abuse at the US, the UN, the OAS, UNESCO, and any other organization which has suggested slowing the rate of growth of the Americas, and preventing the "Central American man from taking firm possession of his land."

The younger elites' confidence in "increased production" as the solution to population problems pales to insignificance when compared with Altamirano's rapturous view of technology:

> Technology makes every inch of land a source of riches. Where a tree cannot grow, something else is produced for man. The craggy mountain peak becomes a site supplying the water or snow producing the electricity which in the hands of man will make bread fall from the heavens, yielding sustenance for all. [*Diario de Hoy*, 13 January 1966].

For one who sees the UN "plagued with agents of international leftism" and the FAO "falling into the hands of the socialist left" it is a short step to viewing family planning as another socialist plot:

> The leftists not only are trying to check our social development, socializing and regimenting us prematurely, but are also holding back our population growth. [*Diario de Hoy*, 28 March 1965].

The basic difference is that the population plot is financed by "racists from the US and Nordic Europe . . . who feel there are too many Negroes, Indians, mulattos, and mestizos."

Such attacks in the early and mid-sixties slowed the pace and aggressiveness of the Salvadoran Demographic Association, founded in 1963. Toward the end of the decade, however, leftist opposition began to mobilize, partly in order to capitalize on the loud and clear policy on population enunciated by North American leaders. A young doctor who frequently gives lectures for the association, describes one form of the leftist opposition:

> The rightist priest never leaves his church. The leftist priest does. Also lay leftists, many of them foreigners—Chileans, Argentines, Belgians, and Brazilians—arrive as trained groups to our meetings and raise captious questions, like "Doctor, I know a woman who was taking the pill and it gave her a heart attack. Is it true that the pills do that?" and "Is it true that the gringos put chemicals in the milk they send here to sterilize the women?"

As in Honduras, however, the principal opposition stems from the university. As phrased by Professor Slutzky of the National University:

> A development policy resting on a decline in birth rates as a mechanism to achieve an improvement in living conditions is condemned to failure since there is no connection between these two phenomena. Why then is there so much emphasis on fertility reduction? Because there are objectives quite foreign to raising living standards. The US utilizes family planning internally in poor areas and in areas of the exploited minorities. Capitalism needs internal colonies. Of course the integration of poverty areas like Chicago or the rural South would imply

structural changes and a redistribution of political power; so the increase in the poor constitutes a political danger when violence is initiated.

The author goes on to charge the OAS with initiating massive sterilization programs, and cites an October, 1968, article in VISPERA, a magazine published in Uruguay by the International Catholic Students Association. It refers to an alleged 1967 campaign on the part of Protestant missionaries in Brazil to distribute IUDs to the Indians.

> One of the objectives of this campaign was demographic control of the natives in order to favor the pacific installation of foreign industries. But we should not ignore the intention too of preparing the Amazon region for colonization by excess Negroes exported by the US.

> Research recently undertaken by Dr. Luis Pérez proved that powdered milk distributed free by the North Americans in maternal and child health programs in Minas Gerais contained contraceptive chemicals.

At the medical school we tried to meet with two young revolutionaries on the staff. One refused to talk to us, the other guardedly explained his position:

> The government, after the Honduran conflict, decided that the nation's problems would be solved by "controllist" means, since over 50,000 people returned to El Salvador. Birth control alone can only help to maintain the status quo. It will maintain the system by reducing existing tensions. Why else would the US be putting so much money into it? Anyway, the rural worker who earns a dollar a day can't plan his family. Family planning adjusts the number of children to the income. By that standard the peasants would have *no* children!

While it might appear that such arguments are just so much rhetoric or purely academic, they have profound influences on policies and programs both within the university and without. A good example of the impact on the social sciences is provided by the story of a young ex-faculty member, one of a handful of five Salvadorans with modern academic training in his discipline:

> I have been interested in family planning for some time and when I finished my training and began to teach at the university I encouraged the students to do small research projects on the structure of the family, including the relation to family planning. I also collaborated with the National Family Planning Association.

> At that time political power in the university was in the hands of students of the extreme left, who began to oppose this kind of research with the usual arguments—violent changes would not be precipitated if family planning were encouraged. Of course these students were practicing it themselves, but they argue that as intellectuals their participation is different from that of the worker or the peasant, for whom the situation must become bad enough to foment revolution.

> In addition, they insisted that the social sciences should be exclusively theoretical, that field research "hypertrofied" students' minds and was a Yanqui import.

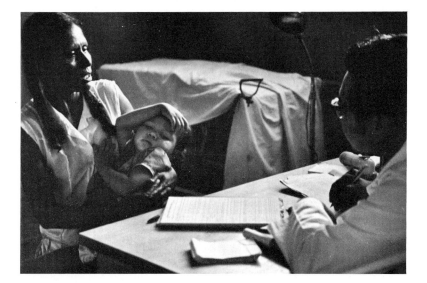

Finally, the university authorities told me I'd have to quit my family-planning activities. I thought this was unethical, and I resigned.

The impact on the medical school has been even more profound. Collaboration with the Family Planning Association in medical training programs has ceased, and an official told us: "We had hoped to add demography to the curriculum, but not now. They even regard the biology of reproduction as a 'smoke screen.'" The issue began to get hot in 1969, and the medical school issued a five-page pronouncement in March of that year entitled "The School of Medicine and Family Planning." While it defined family planning as part of maternal and child health and therefore an appropriate (but not essential) aspect of the physician's duties, it added the following caveat:

> The faculty emphatically declares itself against any birth control program imposed by the state or any other autonomous or semiautonomous agency, since the nation has not carried out a demographic study demonstrating the necessity of an anti-natalist policy.

The most serious consequence of the university stance on family planning occurred as the result of a strike in which the leftist students won a crucial point in their negotiations with the Ministry of Health. The ministry had gradually been absorbing the family-planning clinics of the private association. In the rural areas most of the health clinics are staffed by young MDs putting in their "social service" as a return for the support of their education. The strike established the principle that it will be *up to the physician* to decide whether or not he will participate in the program. "The government MD who doesn't want to give family planning services doesn't have to now," we were told by someone who had just visited most of the rual clinics. "In eight places they have discontinued the service, in others they are slowing the services down by passive resistance, insistence on the medical complications of contraception, and lack of promotion. And yet the private association is pulling out and letting the government take over." Increasingly the university will be a bottleneck to the program, as it graduates physicians technically ill-informed and ideologically opposed to family planning.

The private association is dynamic, believes in what it is doing, and has imaginative outreach programs. It has everything the government has not, except access to the people, and it is gradually phrasing out. While it was attracting close to a thousand new cases per month in early 1969, by August of 1970 the figure had declined to 630. The government program in the same month showed 773 new patients, not even up to the level of the private program in 1969. All agencies combined, including the Social Security hospitals, are running about 24,000 new cases per year.

These are mainly urban women. An unknown proportion would have practiced birth control without the clinics, and perhaps half of those who come in fail to come back. There are close to 700,000 women of reproductive age in El Salvador.

What about the public demand for birth control? Urban surveys indicate that the average woman wants about three children and is interested in family planning, but the intensity of motivations is probably not great. Many women who say they want no more children can easily find rationalizations for having more. A Honduran mother who was unhappy about her pregnancy and wanted no more children also said to us, "That's what God gives us, children. They are the capital that we have." And a poor farmer said, "Many children are a big problem at first but tomorrow if they are good and if they are lucky they can be a help. If they come out good it's a blessing from God."

> "How many children do you want?"
> "I've never thought of that because that is as God wishes. I have three."
> "What about pills?"
> "I've never been interested in them. Even if you're poor you should have the children God sends, you have to work, to look for a way to support them, better children, better citizens."

The origin of such notions is probably not the Catholic Church per se, but a blend of religious and folk beliefs. At any rate, Madre Marta, a nun working in a rural area of Honduras, has a very different notion of parental responsibility:

> God hasn't told us "Accept all the children God sends." That's a false idea they have. The parents have to decide how many they want according to their ability to give food and education to them, so they won't be children lost in the street, dying of hunger. We must educate them that God never said, "You are going to have 8 or 10 children."

The net effect of contradictory feelings about family size is not opposition to family-planning programs, but a kind of moderate interest. If the facilities are made available, without fanfare or promotional activity, there will be a response adequate to satisfy the busy physician essentially interested in other health programs of higher priority, but it will do little to affect national demographic trends.

Conclusion

Unlike Europeans who slowly and painfully invented the modern industrial world, Latin Americans came upon it rather suddenly; almost, one might say, just after World War II, when it became clear to many Latins that other people lived much better than they did. "The mass media raised the levels of aspirations of their audience," explains Torcuato di Tella. "Radio, the cinema, the ideals of the rights of man in written constitutions all tend to produce effects greater than those produced in the European experience."

Moreover, they had some reason to think a miracle was possible when they saw the gifts pouring into European recovery. In the six years following the war, $24 billion in aid went to Europe from the United States, most of it in the form of grants. Unfortunately, Latin America was not to share in such assistance, since, as General Marshall put it, "between Europe in agony and a merely poor Latin America, we are compelled to give priority to Europe." Since Latin America was "merely poor" the remedy consisted of stepping up US investments to the extent that by 1963 American business had $13 billion invested in Latin America. While less than our investments in Canada alone, it might be expected that this amount of money would have highly salutary economic consequences. In fact, since most US money is in petroleum and ores, its impact on employment has been negligible, and its consequences for industrialization far less than the dollar value might suggest. Local capital, on the other hand, went heavily into the export crops which dominate the economies of most Latin American nations, making them highly vulnerable to the vagaries of price fluctuations. Thus a drop of one cent in the price of coffee means $50 million to more than a dozen countries. What this means for the people is described by Victor Alba: "When the price of raw materials rise, the masses live no better than before, but when they fall, the oligarchs contrive to have the cost of the drop, or most of it, paid by the masses, through taxes, subsidies (which the masses pay for) or inflation. . . . When the Korean War caused raw-material prices to rise . . . in Brazil and other coffee-producing countries, there was no change in the living standards of the people; the only change was the increase in the coffee barons' bank deposits in the United States and Switzerland."

Latin Americans feared that North Americans' heavy emphasis on European development would further exacerbate their colonial conditions by keeping them as exporters of raw materials, as importers of manufactured goods, and increasingly dependent upon US investments for capital. Under the forceful leadership of Raul Prebisch, the United Nations Economic Commission for Latin America (ECLA) pushed hard for the development of local industries, protective tariffs, import controls, and foreign public-sector loans rather than foreign investments.

15
Latin America and the United States of America

. . . The Alliance for Progress is dead, however much I should hope for its resurrection. The main reason for its failure seems to be the following: it was necessary to establish close co-ordination between the help from the Alliance and the basic reforms, but unfortunately the rich in Latin America talk too much about reform and label as Communists all those who try to enforce it. This is easy to understand: the rich in Latin America go on holding 80 percent of the land. Often they control parliament and have the intensity of their idealism and hope in the future gauged by the bank deposits kept in their names in the United States and Europe.

ARCHBISHOP DOM HELDER CAMARA, 1963

In the words of Washington observer Peter Nehemkis, "ECLA was for years shunned as an international pariah. It was looked upon by official Washington as an organization whose philosophy was alien to the free enterprise conception of economic development." Prebisch also tried to promote the economic integration of Latin America, a long unrealized dream of Latin American intellectual and political leaders such as Alberdi and Francisco Morazán. Such ideas fell on hostile ears during the Eisenhower administration, but gradual progress was made, especially with regard to Central America.

General economic conditions continued to deteriorate. Prebisch noted that between 1930 and 1960 the per capita index of exports in 1950 dollars had declined from $58 to $39. With few foreign outlets for industrial products and with limited local demand from the impoverished masses, industries in most countries were growing at rates far below urban population growth, while the rural population was growing faster than the number of agricultural jobs. The sorry agricultural situation has been succinctly described by Solon Barraclough: "Agricultural production in Latin America as a whole has actually fallen by about 10 percent per capita from estimated pre-World War II levels; it has just barely kept pace with population growth during the last two decades. Individual country data show Mexico to be the only notable exception to this general picture of relative stagnation."

North Americans suddenly became aware of the buildup of hostility when Vice President Richard Nixon's 1958 visit produced dramatically negative responses. Soon after, the Brazilans urged an *operacion Panamericana* on a United States fearful, according to Roberto Campos, "that the endorsement of the planning philosophy might encourage or hasten state-minded or socialist tendencies in Latin American governments, thus stifling private enterprise." President Kubitschek of Brazil based his sweeping proposals heavily on ECLA recommendations, and emphasized the need for integrated economic planning and objective-quantifiable economic targets—revolutionary concepts for Washington's guardians of laissez faire economics, and fully accepted only when the administration became Democratic and the Cubans veered to the Left.

On March 13, 1961, President Kennedy called the Latin American ambassadors to the White House to announce "a vast effort, unparalleled in magnitude and nobility of purpose, to satisfy the basic needs of the American peoples for homes, work and lands, health and schools." The Alliance for Progress was enthusiastically received by Latin Americans. Liberals were pleased with Washington's acceptance of economic planning and the playing down of private enterprise; rightists, terrified of Cuban-type explosions in their own countries, decided that the

Venezuela

Venezuela

time for social reforms had arrived; and leaders of all persuasions took the goals with a grain of salt. Tad Szulc, citing a "perspicacious Latin American statesman," wrote that "the United States failed to realize the incredible difficulties lying ahead of the Alliance, while the Latin Americans, realizing them fully because they knew themselves and their problems, signed the commitments for self-help and reform without much intention of seriously living up to them."

Certainly the goals as set out by the Punta del Este charter were bold and precise. Among them were "to wipe out illiteracy . . . and assure all children in Latin America by 1970 of at least six years of primary education"; increasing life expectancy by "a minimum of five years"; no less than 2.5 percent per capita annual economic growth; "comprehensive agrarian reform"; and "housing programs to provide decent homes for all our people." While the Alliance moved Latin America forward somewhat toward integration, and introduced rational economic planning elements to a number of governments which had been largely innocent of planning, the relentless decay of economic and social conditions proceeded as if the Alliance had never existed. By 1965 Victor Alba could state categorically: "This fact, whether expressed in Marxist terms, Keynesian terms, ECLA terms, or theosophical terms, may be reduced to a single clear point: Latin America is moving backward. . . . With four years now gone by . . . the existence of Latin Americans today is worse than it was five or ten or fifteen years ago." Perhaps, as Roberto Campos put it, "the Alliance began a few minutes before midnight" and consequently had only a slight possibility of accomplishing anything. There are signs that with the death of President Kennedy the scheme reverted to older patterns. "It soon lapsed," writes Peter Nehemkis, "into an American assistance-granting agency, which spent almost half its capital on emergency transfusions to meet balance of payment crises."

The shift to loans from the United States and from international agencies, while good for programatic flexibility and autonomy, began to cause severe drains on Latin American capital. The external debt of Latin American countries increased from $4 billion in 1955 to $10.6 billion in 1964. American experts began to see the irony in a Marshall Plan consisting of grants which should have been loans, and an Alliance consisting of loans which should have been grants. Along with an increasingly onerous debt service, Latin America continued on the short end of American investments. According to ECLA estimates, $2.8 billion moved from the United States to Latin America in the way of private investments between 1960 and 1966, but $8.3 billion in profits and income returned to the United States.

Ecuador

Meanwhile, US political machinations did little to increase confidence in North American aims. Our aid program seemed continually to have both economic and political strings attached to it, and direct intervention in Cuba and the Dominican Republic merely confirmed the image of the stick poised close to the carrot. The military assistance program further intensified hostility on the part of groups dedicated to making basic changes. The pretense of supplying arms for defense against outside aggression was abandoned. "Emphasis shifted," as Robert McNamara put it in 1963, "to internal security capabilities for use against communist-inspired subversion or overt aggression and to civic action projects designed to promote stability and strengthen national economies." Not only has this helped to entrench many existing regimes, but it has helped to increase intrahesmispheric tensions. "In the last thirty years," said Raul Prebisch recently, "I have not seen one attempt on the American part or any initiative on the Latin American part to arrive at an arms limitation agreement." Senator Frank Church recently said that "the war between El Salvador and Honduras we made possible, in large part, by our gift of arms and training eagerly extended to both sides."

By the mid-sixties it was clear to everyone that neither the objective goals nor the spirit of the Alliance were any longer in sight; that United States political and military muscle was as evident as ever; and that Latin America was adding a huge debt service to its sea of troubles. Little wonder that Lyndon Johnson's 1965 announcement that "less than five dollars invested in population control is worth a hundred dollars invested in economic growth" was greeted with suspicion. Latin Americans, not yet even aware they had a population problem, were convinced that Washington was trying to buy them off with pills—and at an exchange rate of 100 to 5 at that. A subsequent statement by Robert McNamara from his vantage point as World Bank president was widely interpreted as meaning that financial aid would be conditional on Latin acceptance of birth control programs. The Cubans made political hay of the issue throughout Latin America, while neglecting to mention their low birth rate and their unusually extensive birth control services, developed after the revolution. All in all, the United States and Latin America ended the decade of the Alliance for Progress with a most tenuous alliance and a minimum of progress.

El Salvador

The population of Latin America in 1900 took 40 years to double; the population of 1930 doubled by 1960; and the population of 1950 will have doubled by 1975. In the two countries we have chosen as our microcosm, El Salvador and Honduras, the stark implications of such growth for the labor force can be seen. At the time the Alliance was launched in the early 1960s the combined labor force of these countries was growing at about 46,000 persons per year,* but by the middle of the current decade they will be adding 116,000 per year.

If the "green revolution" moves to these countries, will it help? Unfortunately, as has proven true with most Latin American programs of irrigation, colonization, land reclamation, and agricultural credit, it may help *agriculture* but do nothing for the small farmer who makes up most of the agricultural population. The new crop varieties require just what the small farmer doesn't have—capital—for irrigation, fertilizers, and risk taking. As usual, it will be the medium and large farmers who profit, squeezing out even more small farmers to flee to the already clogged cities.

We have tried to show that virtually every problem of Latin America is compounded and exacerbated by population growth. At the same time it should be clear that if population growth stopped tomorrow, none of Latin America's problems would be solved—they simply would not continue getting worse at so rapid a rate. The magnitude and range of Latin America's problems are such that they must be attacked on many fronts in order to make any difference at all.

North-East Brazil

Rising expectations, rapid population growth, and stagnating economic opportunities have combined to create massive dissatisfactions in Latin America—dissatisfactions which are vaguely felt by many, but most dramatically articulated by courageous groups of university students, militant priests, and peasant leaders. Articulate dissatisfaction may be a necessary condition for the solution of social problems, but the solutions themselves are neither evident nor simple to achieve. On the one hand are the utopian revolutionaries who believe that a realignment of wealth and power will at once exploit the jungles and triumph over human injustice; on the other hand are the moderate reformists whose faith lies in the magic of some particular element of modernization, be it mass education, agricultural technology, or community development. Somewhere in between are those who want to do something but simply do not know where to begin. Acutely aware of problems but baffled as to solutions, they react with the puzzled frustration of Salvadoran coffee grower Romulo Leal: "In the last twenty years our population has doubled and the poor people who are marginal to the culture, marginal to material goods, who have no means to defend themselves in the new rhythm of life of the nation. . . . These humble people I see growing poorer every day. Now the solution to this problem, sincerely, I cannot see from any side."

El Salvador

Bolivia

El Salvador

Dominican Republic

Peru

Peru

North-East Brazil

Honduras

Bolivia

A Moderate Solution

I believe that the training of the population together with a progressive policy by the government, can resolve many problems within a decade. Other countries have unexploited, natural wealth such as huge forests, fertile soils, large rivers, minerals, or a fantastic geographic location. El Salvador has absolutely nothing. We have little land and at the same time are over populated; we have a coastline only on the Pacific; and there are no minerals of any kind. In other words, there is no wealth other than the people, and this very population can be a terrible ballast towards progress—if it consumes without producing—or it can be an extraordinary wealth if it produces with efficiency. . . .

We had to decide whether to invest in an economic infrastructure of the traditional type, big highways and so on, or in an intensive exploitation of our human resources. We decided on the latter, so the only solution is to give full priority to education, but education interlocked with economic development, not as an abstract thing for the purpose of intellectual satisfaction.

This is very difficult because we start from zero. The educational system was dreadful, and simply increasing services will lead us nowhere. In El Salvador, as in many parts of Latin America, the educational system has been pointed towards values that have no bearing on Latin America of the twentieth century. We also found that the whole educational system was geared toward a small group preparing to enter the university. Whoever did not enter the university was considered to be a failure.

For many years, in part influenced by UNESCO, we were told that the priority was literacy, that to teach reading and writing was the most important thing; but how does this affect the GNP of a country? The relationship between economic and educational development occurs only after secondary education; so we are beginning to emphasize secondary education—making it more technical, keeping it from being purely humanistic, professionalizing it. So we are now trying out a system of teaching the whole secondary curriculum through television. An elementary school teacher, specially trained for a year, is perfectly capable of teaching up to the ninth grade with the aid of television. By putting television to work we can raise the number of years of compulsory schooling from six to nine. We will be the first in Latin America to do so.

While some say we should first develop the industry and later educate the people, we will first educate the people, and take the risk that the industry will be there to receive them. We have closed our teacher-training schools entirely, and are retraining those already in the service.

I do not wish to give solutions now, nor pretend to solve the next decade's problems. I am working toward preparing a new consciousness among the young, and the product of that new consciousness should be of a high order. I cannot with my present mentality give solutions to a mentality that will take place ten years from now. They will produce the solution!

In knowing how to reason, lies the clue to all!

Walter Beneke,
Minister of Education,
El Salvador, 1970

A Revolutionary Solution

Our generation begins by refusing to accept as given the misery and backwardness of our nation; by rejecting social injustice, and by rejecting the notion that a group of corrupt politicians whether in the barracks, the US embassy, or the Pentagon can decide our country's future. . . . If truly democratic channels are created, the people will follow them, but if crime, fraud, and violence continues, our generation will have to respond with violent revolution. . . . Once the Honduran is again owner of his lands, his mines, his forests and his seas, the fantastic energy and creative capacity of the Honduran people will be liberated to struggle against poverty and underdevelopment.

It will then be possible to exploit empty lands and raw materials to feed and clothe our people, to conquer illiteracy; to people again our forests; to build roads traversing mountains, jungles and swamps; to build dams to supply energy and irrigation water. We will conquer the underpopulated jungles and marshes by new generations of *campesinos* from overpopulated areas. The poor boys who now sell newspapers, suffer from hunger, and sleep in the streets will enjoy education and the warmth of a home.

In building a new Honduras, the role of university students is in study and, even more, in action. . . . With all its dangers and sacrifices, revolutionary activity is required, . . . helping to make other students and the general public aware of the problem of university and nation. . . .

. . . The true revolutionary will create a new Honduras, reflecting the effort, tenacity and spirit of struggle and sacrifice characteristic of today's youth.

**From *Economía Política*,
a journal of the Economics Faculty
of the University of Honduras, November, 1969**

Stunned by the Cuban experience and pressured by the U.S., many conservative Latin American governments, at the end of the 1961 Punta del Este Economic Conference, subscribed to the proposition that it would be safer to bear some sort of land reform than to court peasant revolution . . . the experts agree that what is being done is too little, too late, too costly, too badly planned and executed, and these "reforms" are simply insufficient to keep up with the natural growth of the population, let alone redistribute the land or break the rural power structure.

RODOLFO STAVENHAGEN

Bibliography

Alba, Victor. *Alliance Without Allies*. New York: Frederick A. Praeger, 1965.

Américas, September, 1969. "OAS Halts War Between El Salvador and Honduras." Washington, 1969.

Asociación de Estudiantes de Humanidades. *Contribución al Estudio del Conflicto Hondureño*. San Salvador: Departamento de Ciencias Sociales, Facultad de Humanidades, Universidad de El Salvador, 1969.

Barraclough, Solon L. "Agricultural Policy and Strategies of Land Reform," in *Masses in Latin America*, edited by I. L. Horowitz. New York: Oxford University Press, 1970.

Campos, Roberto de Oliveira. *Reflections on Latin American Development*. Austin: University of Texas Press, 1967.

Chinchilla Cuellar, J. A. "Patología Quirúrgica en el Centro de Salud de Chalatenango." M.D. dissertation, Salvadoran School of Medicine, 1970.

Chonchol, Jacques. "Land Tenure and Development in Latin America," in *Obstacles to Change in Latin America*, edited by Claudio Véliz. London: Oxford University Press, 1965.

Church, Frank. "Toward a New Policy for Latin America," in *Conscientization for Liberation*, edited by L. M. Colonnese. Washington, U.S. Catholic Conference, 1971.

Consejo Nacional de Planificación y Coordinación Económica. "Cuantificación y Análisis de la Población Salvadoreña Expulsada de Honduras." San Salvador, 1969.

Consejo Nacional de Planificación y Coordinación Económica. *Plan de La Nación para el Desarrollo Económico y Social 1965–69*. San Salvador, 1964.

Direccion General de Estadística y Censos, Honduras. *Estadísticas Educacionales, 1967*. Tegucigalpa, 1969.

di Tella, Torcuato. "Populism and Reform in Latin America," in *Obstacles to Change in Latin America*, edited by Claudio Véliz. London: Oxford University Press, 1965.

Estudios Centro-Americanos, Numero 254–255 extraordinario. "El Conflicto Honduras—El Salvador." San Salvador: Universidad José Simeón Cañas, 1969.

Frank, Andrew G. "Urban Poverty in Latin America," in *Masses in Latin America*, edited by I. L. Horowitz. New York: Oxford University Press, 1970.

Gavidia, José Manuel. "Factores Económicos y Salud Rural en El Salvador." M.D. dissertation, Salvadoran School of Medicine, 1964.

Illich, Iván. "The False Ideology of Schooling." *Saturday Review*, 17 October 1970.

Instituto de Investigaciones Económicas y Sociales. *Análisis Sobre el Conflicto Entre Honduras y El Salvador*. Tegucigalpa: Facultad de Ciencias Económicas, Universidad Nacional Autónoma de Honduras, 1969.

International Population Program. *An Assessment of Fertility and an Evaluation of Health and Family Planning Programs in Las Crucitas, Tegucigalpa, Honduras*. Ithaca: Cornell University, International Population Program, 1969.

Mata, C. G.; and Aguilár, V. *Educación y Crecimiento Demográfico en Centroamérica*. Guatemala City: Instituto Centroamericano de Población y Familia, 1968.

Ministerio de Educación, El Salvador. *Diagnóstico Estadístico y Proyecciones de la Educación Primaria en El Salvador*. San Salvador: Ministry of Education, 1970.

Ministerio de Educación, El Salvador. *Plan Quinquenal de Educación*. San Salvador: Ministry of Education, 1970.

Morán de Ferrer, Rhina. "El Aborto en el Hospital de Maternidad." M.D. dissertation, Salvadoran School of Medicine, 1969.

Mundigo, Axel. "Elites, Economic Development and Population." Ph.D. dissertation, Cornell University, 1972.

Nathan, Robert R. Associates. "Agricultural Sectoral Analysis for El Salvador." Universidad de El Salvador, October 1969.

Nehemkis, Peter. *Latin America: Myth and Reality*. New York: The New American Library, 1966.

Organization of American States. "Informe Final del SubComité del CIAP sobre El Salvador." CIAP 414 (9 June 1970).

Pincus, Joseph. "The Effects of Industrialization on Salaried Employment, Hours and Wages in Industry in El Salvador." Report to AID Mission in El Salvador. August 1968 (mimeo).

Pozas, Ricardo. "La Organización de Cooperativas de Producción Agropecuaria en Honduras, C.A." *Revista Mexicana de Sociología*, XXIX, No. 1, January–March, 1967.

Prebisch, Raúl. Comment reported in "Military Aid: Bandaid for Latin America." *Center Report*, Center for the Study of Democratic Institutions, 1970.

Prebisch, Raúl. *Transformación y Desarrollo*. Report to the Interamerican Development Bank, Santiago, 1970 (mimeo).

Footnotes

Riba, Jorge Ricardo. *La Vivienda en Centroamérica.* San Salvador: Organización de Estados Centroamericanos, 1969.

Ruiz García, Samuel. "The Latin American Church Since Medellín," in *Conscientization for Liberation,* edited by L. M. Collonese, Washington, U.S. Catholic Conference, 1971.

Salegio, Oscar René. *Análisis de la Situación y del Plan Habitacional de El Salvador.* San Salvador: Instituto de Vivienda Urbana, 1968.

Segal, Aaron. "Mini-War in Central American." *Venture.* London: Fabian Society, October 1969, pp. 21–24.

Slutsky, Daniel. "Política Demográfica y Subdesarrollo en Centroamerica." San Salvador: Universidad de El Salvador, 1969.

Social Progress Trust Fund. *Socio-Economic Progress in Latin America.* Washington, D.C., 1967.

Soto Blanco, Ovidio. *La Educación en Centroamérica.* San Salvador: Organization of Central American States, 1968.

Stares, Rodney C. *The Campesino Economy in the Southern Region of Honduras.* Cholutéca, Honduras, 1970 (mimeo).

Stavenhagen, Rodolfo. "Seven Fallacies About Latin America," in J. Petras and M. Zeitlin, eds., *Latin America, Reform or Revolution.* Greenwich, Connecticut: Fawcett Publications, 1968.

Stycos, J. Mayone. *Human Fertility in Latin America,* Chapter 16, "Education and Fertility in Latin America." Ithaca: Cornell University Press, 1968.

Szulc, Tad. *The Winds of Revolution.* New York: Frederick A. Praeger, 1965.

United Nations Economic Commission of Latin America. *Urbanization in Latin America.* E/CN 12/662 (March 1963).

Wagley, Charles. "The Peasant," in *Continuity and Change in Latin America,* edited by John J. Johnson. Stanford: Stanford University Press, 1964.

White, Robert. "The Radio Schools as an Influence in Political Self-Determination" (unpublished manuscript).

World Health Organization. *World Health Statistics Annual.* Geneva, 1965.

1. Rodney C. Stares, "The Campesino Economy in the Southern Region of Honduras," mimeographed (Choluteca, Honduras, 1970).

2. Ricardo Pozas, "La Organizacion de Cooperativas de Produccion Agropecuria en Honduras, C.A.," *Revista Mexicana de Sociologia* 29:1 (January–March, 1967).

3. Ibid.

4. Samuel Ruiz Garcia, "The Latin American Church Since Medellin," in *Conscientization for Liberation,* ed. L. M. Colonnese (Washington: U.S. Catholic Conference, 1971), p. 85.

5. Robert White, "The Radio Schools as an Influence in Political Self-Determination" (unpublished manuscript).

6. Axel Mundigo, "Elites, Economic Development and Population" (Ph.D. diss., Cornell University, 1971).

7. When 37 Honduran physicians were asked the same question in another Cornell study, 22 said that Honduras's population was "inadequate." Only 8 fully agreed to a national family planning program to reduce the rate of population increase.

8. B. F. Landstreet and A. I. Mundigo, "University Students," in *Ideology, Faith and Family Planning in Latin America,* ed. J. Mayone Stycos (New York: McGraw-Hill, 1971).

9. If we include those who "partially favor" a national program, the percentages rise markedly but the differences remain, from 85 percent of the rightists to 61 percent of the radical leftists.

10. Á. Slutzky, "Politica Demografica y Sub-Desarollo en Centro America" (Universidad del Salvador, Facultad de Ciencias y Humanidades, 1969).

11. This is composed of 69,000 annual entries to the economically active population and 23,000 annual departures due to death or retirement. See "Proyecciones de la Población Economicamente Activa," *CELADE,* Series C (June, 1967).

"In the last twenty years
   our population has doubled
   and the poor people
   who are marginal to the culture,
   marginal to material goods,
   who have no means to defend themselves
   in the new rhythm of life of the nation…
   These humble people I see
   growing poorer every day.
   Now the solution to this problem,
   sincerely, I cannot see from any side."
ROMULO LEAL, SALVADORAN COFFEE GROWER